5 —

ON ESCAPE

Cultural Memory
in
the
Present

Mieke Bal and Hent de Vries, Editors

ON ESCAPE

De l'évasion

Emmanuel Levinas

Translated by Bettina Bergo

STANFORD UNIVERSITY PRESS

STANFORD, CALIFORNIA

Assistance for the translation was provided
by the French Ministry of Culture.

On Escape was originally published in French in 1982
under the title *De l'évasion* © 1982, Fata Morgana.

Stanford University Press
Stanford, California
© 2003 by the Board of Trustees of the
Leland Stanford Junior University

Printed in the United States of America
on acid-free, archival-quality paper

Library of Congress Cataloging-in-Publication Data
Levinas, Emmanuel.
  [De l'évasion. English]
  On escape / Emmanuel Levinas; translated by Bettina Bergo.
    p.   cm.—(Cultural memory in the present)
  ISBN 0-8047-4139-5 (cloth : alk. paper)
  ISBN 0-8047-4140-9 (pbk : alk. paper)
1. Ontology.   I. Title.   II. Series.
BD331.L459613 2003
111—dc21   2002153165

Original Printing 2003
Last figure below indicates year of this printing:
12   11   10   09   08   07   06
Typeset by Robert C. Ehle in 10.5/13.5 Adobe Garamond

Contents

Translator's Acknowledgments

This work would not have been possible without the recommendations, corrections, and support of the following people and institutions.

Michael Nass, DePaul University
Michael Smith, Berry College
François Raffoul, Louisiana State University
Emily Katz, Duquesne University
Lia Brozgal, Harvard University
Richard Boothby, Loyola College (Maryland)
Martin Cohen, (Boston College)
Robert L. Bernasconi, University of Memphis
Judith Vichniac, Radcliffe Institute for
    Advanced Study
Robert Gibbs, University of Toronto
Robert Cohen, Boston University (Emeritus)
Gary M. Shapiro, University of Richmond
Loyola College in Maryland, Humanities Center
Alfred E. Tauber, Center for Philosophy and History
    of Science (Boston University)
The Radcliffe Institute for Advanced Study
    (Harvard University)
The Center for European Studies
    (Harvard University)

ON ESCAPE

Letter from Emmanuel Levinas

Dear Jacques Rolland,

When our friend Bruno Roy proposed, some time ago, a new edition of my study "De l'évasion" [On Escape], published in 1935 in *Recherches Philosophiques*—which was directed by Alexandre Koyré and Albert Spaïer, Jean Wahl, and Gaston Bachelard, and had been an avant-garde philosophical journal in the pre-war years[1]—I did not dare consent. It would certainly have been agreeable to me to have the occasion to evoke these noble, venerated names, and I willingly admitted that my old text was perhaps in a position to bear witness to an intellectual situation of meaning's end, wherein the existence attached to being forgot, on the eve of great massacres, even the problem of its own justification. But, for that, these pages needed notes and commentary, and it seemed to me difficult to interpret my own youth.

You have kindly agreed to take charge of this task of explication, and you have accomplished it in a most remarkable fashion. You have included my modest essay—in which the consciousness of having no way out [*sans-issue*] was tied to a determined anticipation of impossible new thoughts—in the context of great contemporary ideas. You have made major voices resound in counterpoint to my lines, or you transformed them into echoes of great human whispering. Your generous attention has succeeded in extracting from my words—already then growing silent—the forebodings that they still harbored.

Heartfelt thanks to you for so much knowledge, talent, and friendship.

EMMANUEL LEVINAS
DECEMBER 1981

Getting Out of Being by a New Path
Jacques Rolland

"To philosophize: Is this to decipher a hidden writing in a palimpsest?"[1] The task incumbent on us is perhaps the inverse of this. It should consist of reading in an early text the inscription of a future writing—if only obliquely [*en creux*]—of a book "to come," but one that is so little like Blanchot's title that it will indeed come to be. It should be a matter of glimpsing something, as Pushkin did when Onegin and the young Tatiana first appeared to him, albeit in a confused form.

> Through the magic crystal.
> The future of this free novel.[2]

This expresses an attitude whose meaning and import must be specified. It means, first, that we recognize, in the text we are presenting, its status as a "youthful work." But this also means, simultaneously, that the interest one attributes to this text "of youth" is not only that of the historian of philosophy, concerned with reconstituting the stages of a "path of thinking," and therefore devoted to studying the first stage of this path, mainly with a documentary goal in mind. In other words, we should take on this text in the introductory spirit in which it sees itself (57), while specifying exactly what this introductory character means. Let us say, then, that we understand it as an intro-duction and, more precisely, an intro-duction to, and into, the space of questioning in which an investigation subsequently proceeded, one that "remained faithful to its finality, even if it varied in its terminology, its formulas, its operative concepts and certain of its theses."[3] That is, even if, in regard to this text of 1935, the investigation managed above all to give a meaning and direction to that "escape" whose account asserted, at that time, only its pure demand. In a word, this means that we believe we have to do with a text that already belongs to a space of questioning, a text that is therefore philosophically *alive*, and that in publishing it and reading it we are consequently doing something completely different from an archaeology or a palaeography.

The delimitation of this attitude should allow us to define the task of our introduction. It has not seemed to us to be that of an explication, following line by line a text that presents no major technical difficulties. Neither does it seem to us to be that of reconstituting its own movement, or the way in which the analysis leads from one notion to another according to a style [*allure*] particularly characteristic of its author, which in the present case would pass from need to pleasure, from pleasure to shame, from shame to nausea, and from there to escape, whence the analysis had precisely begun.[4] The task of this introduction is thus, instead, to direct us straightaway toward the philosophical problem posed by the pages it attempts to introduce. This problem is raised by the "inimitable theme" (54) the pages have chosen to analyze. Speaking unambiguously: "The need for escape—whether filled with chimerical hopes or not, no matter!—leads us into the heart of philosophy. *It allows us to renew the ancient problem of being qua being*" (56, our emphasis).

And so, two distinct tasks come to light. To begin with, it will be a matter of seeking to situate in this study the signification of the word *being* [*être*]; of questioning ourselves about the will to "renew the ancient problem" when it comes to light in our century in the mid-1930s, and of wondering, finally, what would become of his early comprehension of this concept (being qua being) in the later works. In a second moment, it is up to us to elucidate the demand for "escape" that arises from this way of understanding the verb *to be*, and then to clarify the "program" of philosophical investigation that it announces. In a word, it will be a matter of asking ourselves what this somewhat enigmatic expression, "escape," promises, and of detecting traces of its evolution within the later work.

As we can thus see, the metaphor borrowed from Pushkin will be in play throughout this introduction. Let us therefore specify our position. We think that the meaning of the word *being* [*être*][5] developed in this "youthful" text remains unchanged into the most mature works—even though many related aspects meanwhile undergo essential modifications, like the metaphors chosen to specify being's modes of presence, the situations analyzed to approach its senses, and the modality of the approach itself. We think, on the other hand, that this rather obscure metaphor of escape or evasion, which itself never gets raised to the level of an operative concept, and which, precisely, is here defined neither in its exact meaning (which would no doubt be impossible when Levinas's "phenomenology" shows it precisely to be a need to get out, but which does not desire to go anywhere in particular), nor in its own modalities (one may recall that the essay's final sentence speaks—in terms that were chosen deliberately to give our introduction its title, but also to underscore the preliminary, open, but also indeterminate character of "On Escape"—only of "getting out of being by a new path," without specifying in any way what this path might be), nevertheless opens the path of a thought that is *one* and *whole* [*pensée* une]. And we believe this in spite of the "contradictions" that "the inevitably successive character of all inquiry" largely explains.[6] In a word, we believe that what lies hidden behind this metaphor is the urgent requirement of thinking beyond being, understood in its verbal sense, a requirement that nevertheless will not find adequate philosophical expression until the counter-concept of "otherwise than being" is forged.

  Our introduction will have reached its goal if it is able to fulfill these two tasks. A certain number of notes will help it in this; they accompany the text reprinted here, whose spirit we shall now clarify. It has not seemed useful to us to overburden the text with notes having a merely explicative or technical character, and it is for this reason that we have renounced giving unto Caesar what is his, and unto Bergson what comes from his work, when such specifications would have had only an academic interest. On the other hand, it seemed interesting to us to multiply the references to Levinas's later work, to show how he was able later on to take up, develop, modify, or simply abandon certain of the analyses and intuitions here. In the introduction itself, it appeared essential to us to shed light on what best characterizes the philosophical situation of this study: the latent conflict with Heidegger, whose name, we cannot fail to notice, is never cited in the approximately twenty pages of the first edition.

1. From "Being" to "There Is"

Let us come straight to the question. "The need for escape or evasion leads us into the heart of philosophy. It allows us to renew the ancient problem of being qua being." (56) In thus defining the object of his and of all philosophical investigations, Levinas seems to be stating a great deal—and silencing, or insinuating, still more. In effect, in reading these lines, can we fail to hear those that began a book published barely ten years before, and which found its justification precisely in the necessity, or the urgency, of posing anew the question of the meaning of being: *Being and Time*, a work that Levinas understood from the first in its essential and properly revolutionary dimension, the same Levinas who would, from 1932, devote the first substantial study in French to it?[7] In these lines, the tacit reference to the Heideggerian work is evident, which is far from saying, however, that this reference goes without posing problems. It is therefore fitting that we be fully explicit here—at the risk of being somewhat ponderous in recalling things that are today part of the public domain of philosophical culture—and specify exactly what this reference to Heidegger amounts to or, in a sense, what the debt to Heidegger is.[8] + *debt to Heidegger*

What is, in the first place, taken over from Heidegger without contestation is a certain comprehension of philosophy, by virtue of which one problem will be considered as philosophical par excellence *in as much as* it confronts us with "the ancient problem of being qua being." This means that the problem of philosophy is identically that of being and its meaning or that conversely, and borrowing an expression from Levinas's 1932 study, "the search for meaning, *ontology*, is philosophy itself."[9] And it is again evident that to recognize with

Heidegger that philosophy defines itself by being affixed to [*ar-rimage*] the question of being is at the same time to think being with him in the dimension of the *ontological difference*. This is to take leave of "any thinking that could not distinguish between existence and the existent" (58),[10] that could not make a distinction between "*what is*" and "the *being* of what is," which is understood as "that by which all powers and all properties are posited" (57) or as "the very event of being of all beings."[11] We thereby understand without difficulty that, almost forty years later, in the sort of intellectual autobiography of a whole generation that opens the preface to *Proper Names*, Levinas could write, "And, thanks to Heidegger, our ears have been educated to hear being in its verbal resonance, an unusual and unforgettable sonority."[12] Levinas will retain from Heidegger a third, fundamental thing: the idea that "the being that reveals itself to *Dasein* does not reveal itself in the form of a theoretical notion that one might contemplate."[13] But that its concept can be elaborated only on the basis by which the existence of *Dasein* is made explicit.

And yet it is here, on this terrain with its incontestably Heideggerian aspect, that the question of the meaning of being must be posed or posed again, afresh. Here Levinas proposes to renew the ancient problem of being by posing these few questions, in which the tacit reference to Heidegger immediately takes a polemical turn.

What is the structure of this pure being? Does it have the universality Aristotle conferred on it? Is it the ground and the limit of our preoccupations, as certain modern philosophers would have it? On the contrary, is it nothing else than the mark of a certain civilization, firmly established in the fait accompli of being and incapable of getting out of it? And, in these conditions, is *excendence* [rising out of] possible, and how would it be accomplished? What is the ideal of happiness and human dignity that it promises? (56)[14]

It would seem, then, that the specifications provided in 1947 in Levinas's introduction to *Existence and Existents* also apply to the essay of 1935. "If, at the beginning, our reflections were to a large degree inspired—for their notion of ontology and the relationship that man has with being—by the philosophy of Martin Heidegger, they are driven by a profound need to leave the climate of that philosophy, and by the conviction that we could not leave it for a philosophy qualified as pre-Heideggerian."[15]

A profound need to leave the *climate* of Heideggerian thought, without falling back, all the same, into a thinking that still confuses beings with their being, without falling back, all the same, into what we are today accustomed to calling metaphysics. This was a need that, in this year of 1935, became a "profound need to get out of being" (72) and to that end promoted as an urgency and a demand the task of "renewing the ancient problem of being qua being." A profound need to repeat the question of being, with Heidegger inasmuch as he makes this repetition possible but nevertheless against him in that he appears as the very one who "accepts being" (73) and as the most eminent of "all those who ask only not to go beyond being" (72) because they see in it "the ground and limit of our preoccupations" (56).[16] Yet this is a profound need whose root must be found in the description itself of being, awakened in its verbality or considered as a pure *fact of being*. Levinas's meditation will align itself, in effect, with pure *existence*, with *existentia* or *quoddity*, distinct from *essentia* or *quiddity*. However, in thus aligning itself, the meditation will also stop and tarry there, and in this stopping or this tarrying, it will venture to think existence or existing prior to or without an existent, and thus, as we shall see, to immediately take its distance not only relative to Heidegger, but also starting from him.

Before coming to this point, let us note that Levinas's meditation will thereby encounter a tautology that nevertheless, far from stopping his thought by enclosing it in reduplication, will on the contrary place it on its path and allow it ultimately to realize the project of "renewing the ancient problem of being." It will do this by revealing in being a *defect* or *taint* (56) inscribed in its very fact of existence.

"Being is: there is nothing to add to this assertion as long as we envision in a being only its existence. This reference to oneself is precisely what one states when one speaks of the identity of being. Identity is not a property of being, and it could not consist in the resemblance between properties that, in themselves, suppose identity. Rather, it expresses the sufficiency of the fact of being, whose absolute and definitive character no one, it seems, could place in doubt." (51)

In other words, "The fact of being is always already perfect" (57). But it is worth understanding again that this "perfection" is of a quite particular nature, since one must say simultaneously that "the fact of being is placed beyond the distinction between the perfect and the imperfect" (51), and soon that "being is 'imperfect' inasmuch as it is being, and not inasmuch as it is finite being" (69). The "perfection" of being is not commensurable with that of beings, and this is why it is placed beyond the distinction of the perfect and the imperfect, just as it is placed beyond the distinction of the finite and the infinite. The "perfection" of being is "the elementary truth that *there is being*" when this truth "is revealed at a depth that measures its brutality and its seriousness" (52).

The "perfection" of being is its brutality, the brutality of its *there is* [*il y a*].[17] This perfection is, in effect, that of a verb, of being's pure verbality, that is, again, its pure *affirmation*. Being is: the proposition does not get past the tautology, but in the tautology itself, the proposition signifies that being is affirmed or posited; it signifies, one might say, *being's energy of being*. These are perfect assertions and positions, inasmuch as they are not those of a being, but rather designate the verb *through* which alone beings may be posited. This is the case inasmuch as they designate the very fact of affirmation or position, the fact that *there is* [*il y a*], on the in-side or withdrawn from all *that which is*, the fact by which there is all that there is. But this is, simultaneously—and it will be the task of this study to show it—an imperfect assertion or position, essentially imperfect because horrible in the way they have of asserting themselves without reserve or positing themselves to the point of imposing absolutely. This is a "perfect" energy in its kind but an essentially "imperfect" one in the logic of its functioning.

Yet this defect, simultaneously designated as perfection and imperfection, cannot be made explicit by the contemplation of being as a theoretical object. This is only possible through the elucidation of the relationship that beings [*un étant*] have to this pure being [*être pur*], that is, beings that always have some form of relationship to being, such that they always also have a certain comprehension of being. It is in the intrigue, tied up between man and being, and there alone, that something can be said about this being; it is in this existence, and through certain modalities that affect it and give it its savor and its nuances, that the philosophical, or ontological, meditation finds its point of departure. In Levinas's essay on escape, the feeling that allows both an initial approach to the problem of being and the qualification of the modality through which human beings relate to it is defined as "*the acute feeling of being held fast*" (52; Rolland's emphasis). It is worth our while to read the lines that follow the words we just cited. The "impossibility of getting out of the game and of giving back to things their toy-like uselessness heralds the precise instant at which infancy comes to an end and defines the very notion of seriousness. What counts, then, in all this experience of being, is the discovery not of a new characteristic of our existence, but of its very fact, the very permanent quality [*l'inamovibilité*] of our presence" (52).

It is therefore not merely in human existing that the "ancient problem of being qua being" is put in question and the path of its renewal opened; it is, more precisely, in this human existing *becoming aware of its own existence, of the very fact of this existence, and of the irrevocable quality of its presence.* These are observations that, if we are to grasp this text, cannot fail to lead us again outside the text we are introducing, toward the thought to which Levinas had, a few years earlier, introduced French readers when he published "Martin Heidegger et l'ontologie" ["Martin Heidegger and Ontology"]. This thought refers evidently to Heidegger's notion of *Geworfenheit* ["throwness"].[18] We will therefore cite *in extenso* Levinas's 1932 study, allowing ourselves to be awakened, on our side, in reading it by the use of terms that will make a decisive return in his 1935–36 essay, notably, *being held fast*, the nonremovable or permanent presence, *fact*, and so on.

Dasein understands itself in a certain affective disposition (*Befindlichkeit*). At first sight, this might seem to be a matter of the phenomenon whose superficial aspect classical psychology targets in saying that every state of consciousness is colored by an affective tonality: good or bad humor, joy, boredom, fear, etc. But, for Heidegger, these dispositions cannot be states: they are *modes of self-understanding*, that is to say, *of being there* [*ici-bas*].[19]

But affective disposition, whose understanding is in no way detached from it, shows us its fundamental character. The affective disposition shows us the fact that *Dasein* is riveted to its possibilities, that its "there" [*ici-bas*] is imposed on it. In existing, *Dasein* is always already thrown *into the midst* of its possibilities and not placed before them. It has always already grasped or missed them. Heidegger captures *this fact* of being thrown into the midst of one's own possibilities and of being abandoned to them by the term "Geworfenheit" [thrownness], which we translate more liberally by the term "dereliction" [*déréliction*]. Dereliction is the source and necessary foundation of affectivity. Affectivity is a phenomenon comprehensible only there where existence presents this structure of being delivered over to its own destiny.

Dereliction, as abandonment to imposed possibilities, gives to human existence its character of a *fact* in the strongest and most dramatic sense of the term, in relation to which the empirical facts of the sciences are but derivative: it is a fact that is understood as such by its facticity. Having been thrown into the world, abandoned and delivered over to oneself—such is the ontological description of a fact. Human existence and the positive characteristics of human finitude and nothingness . . . are defined, for Heidegger, by facticity (*Faktizität*). And the understanding and interpretation of this facticity is itself the analytic ontology of *Dasein*. That is why Heidegger and his followers define ontology as a "hermeneutics of facticity (*Hermeneutik der Faktizität*)."[20]

It is perhaps fitting to understand "On Escape" as such an essay on the hermeneutics of facticity, one that nevertheless differs immediately from Heidegger's interpretation by stopping at greater length at *Geworfenheit*, which translates the *fact*, for *Dasein*, of being *riveted* to its possibilities, more readily than it does a dereliction with overly existentialist overtones. Likewise, we noted above that the thinking stops and tarries with the consideration of existence or pure existing [*de l'existence ou de l'exister pur*], that is, existence prior to or without existents. Here, this pause, effected with the meditation on *Geworfenheit*, as the fact of being riveted, is translated by a halt in the movement of Heidegger's meditation itself. To understand this, let us first read the rest of the analysis given in 1932.

But if the understanding of possibilities by *Dasein* is characterized as its dereliction, this existence, precisely qua understanding of possibilities, contains in it a propensity to go beyond the situation imposed. *Dasein* finds itself always already beyond itself. . . . This way of being thrown forward toward one's own possibilities, of adumbrating [*esquisser*] them by way of existence itself, is a fundamental moment of understanding and Heidegger sets it down using the word *Entwurf*, which we translate as "projecting" [*projet-esquisse*].[21]

One might say that Levinas's reflection will remain at *Geworfenheit* for a moment, in order to discover and describe a situation in which existence no longer finds in itself a propensity to go forth beyond the situation imposed, a situation in which *being-thrown* paralyzes, in some way, every possibility of *projecting oneself.*

We will attempt to read the "Hermeneutic of facticity,"[22] here, not in relation to *Being and Time*, but instead to a work far more comparable from the point of view of its dimensions, i.e., Heidegger's seminar "What Is Metaphysics?" [*Was ist Metaphysik?*][23] A hermeneutic that will be conducted thanks to the analysis of a disposition (*Stimmung*) in which this *Geworfenheit* or this fact-of-being-thrown-into [*fait-d'être-jeté-dans*], and this facticity or fact-of-being-already-there [*fait-d'être-déjà-là*] will be shown in all their breadth and all their signification, and which will consequently merit consideration as a fundamental disposition (*Grundstimmung*). The latter is not boredom, which "manifests the being in its totality" (*Was ist Metaphysik?*, pp. 30/50/56). But neither is it "the joy felt in the presence of the being-there . . . of the being we love" (WM 30/50/56). It is not dread or fear (*Furcht*), which is always a fear before and for something determinate (WM 31/51/58). But neither is it *anxiety*, which Heidegger's seminar considers to be precisely the *Grundstimmung* (WM 31/51/57) and which differs initially from fear by virtue of its fundamentally indeterminate character (WM 32/51/58). The fundamental disposition manifesting being qua being, which is announced in the feeling of being riveted or held fast is *nausea.* ✳

One specification is needed here. In *Being and Time* and *What Is Metaphysics?*, anxiety no more had a psychological sense than nausea has a purely and simply physiological one in *On Escape*. To be brief, and since we benefit from hindsight, let us say without further ado that it is on the basis of what nausea would become in Sartre's prose that it should here be understood.[24] For Sartre, the feeling of nausea has its origin in the fact that a glass of beer on a café table, the odious lavender suspenders of the café owner, the roots of a chestnut tree plunging into the earth in a public garden, a simple flat pebble that is, no doubt, humid and muddy on one side, and altogether dry (and thus in no way "nauseating") on the other—suddenly *exist*. They exist in such a way that they somehow melt into this existence or this being that alone remains, while what constituted them as manipulable things or knowable things, things utilizable or admirable, fades away: the form that assembled their "qualities" and presented them in a face (εἶδος). In brief, it is in its ontological significance, or as a *Stimmung* in Heidegger's sense, that nausea must be understood.

Yet a difficulty of principle seems to oppose our *rapproche-ment* between anxiety and nausea. In effect, the former is char-acterized—as we have already emphasized—by its essential *in-determination.* But it certainly seems, on the other hand, that something quite determinate gives rise, each time, to nausea. Speaking medically or physiologically, the cause of nausea is al-ways effectively a something, a something determinate or ther-apeutically determinable. Whether it is a matter of the view of a particularly repugnant spectacle, the diffusion of an especially disheartening odor, or the absorption of a toxic substance, the origin of nausea is always, at least in principle, medically iden-tifiable. Nonetheless, the medical diagnosis is not yet a phe-nomenological analysis! What is in fact important to know here is simply whether nausea, *in its phenomenon,* can let itself be circumscribed as readily as anxiety, and in a general sense, whether it allows itself to be led back to its determinate "cause." No doubt, nausea can be considered the symptom of a hepatic imbalance, whose origin it is medicine's task to deter-mine. But the determination of nausea as a symptom, whose cause must be "diagnosed" and "treated," concerns only the ob-jective gaze—or at least the already objectivizing gaze, which is liable, precisely, to consider nausea a symptom in order to take interest in it qua medical gaze, or to worry about it qua mater-nal gaze. On the other hand, all this could not concern him who, "having nausea," feels simply "caught in an atrocious fun-nel," according to Rimbaud's arresting expression in *Les assis* [The Seated Ones].[25] All this in no way concerns the nausea considered in its phenomenality or "when considered in the in-stant in which it is lived, and in the atmosphere that surrounds it" (66). No one who is sick at heart or whose "innards heave" [*qui a "mal au cœur"*] has ever cared to know whether he had, at that moment, a "liver disease"! No doubt, he might do so afterward, and no doubt he ought to do so if he cares about his health; but while he "is nauseated" [*a la nausée*], he simply and only has "heaving *innards*" or is "sick at *heart*" [*mal au cœur*]. An admirable expression! How could the viscera in question in the physiological process have the slightest importance for one who simply "wants to vomit"? In that instant without a future "that precedes vomiting, and from which vomiting will deliver us" (66), and without nausea itself having any awareness of this promise, we are sick at *heart* in such a way that it is the heart, or the depths of ourselves, that is touched, but in this way, too, our whole being is affected in its manner of existing or relating to its own existence. In this way, that before which nausea is born is only determined for an external eye, whereas this determinate quality has totally disappeared—or rather had never been present—for one who is caught in the trap of nausea. *By the same right* as anxiety, nausea is characterized by an essential indeterminacy, that is, an indeterminacy "that is nonetheless not the simple lack of determinacy, but the essential impossibility of receiving a determination of some sort" (WM, 32/51/58).

Now that this principial difficulty has been removed, we must inquire about what nausea as a *Stimmung*[26] manifests. In order to do this—and for the convenience of this presentation, since the analysis of nausea in its general phenomenon should lead to the same results—we will analyze a particular case of nausea, which is also its origin from the etymological perspective: "seasickness" [*le mal de mer*].[27] It is no doubt a truism to note that when one is at sea, one can have seasickness, but this truism may prove fecund. We have seasickness because we are at sea, that is, off the coast, of which we have lost sight. That is, again, because the earth is gone, the same earth into which, ordinarily, we sink our feet in order, in this position or stance, to exist. Seasickness appears once this loss of the earth is given [*se

donne] as our situation. Seasickness arises when the fact of being at sea is transformed [*se transforme*] into the feeling of having lost our footing in some way, or into a mute and encom-
passing consciousness of having likewise lost *all that is*. For, we
are quite alone when we are at sea, in such a way that we could
be seasick. Not even the boat on which we have embarked
(and, whether it is a launch or a steamer, it is always, at that
moment, a matter of having a nut shell for a hull) appears then
as a thing alongside of which we might be. Seasickness originates precisely when the embarkation disappears as a thing, in
such a way that we are no longer alongside it, but rather form a
single entity [*faisons corps avec*] with it, floating to its rhythm.
That on which we are floating then disappears in its turn qua
sea, to become little more than the pure element upon which
we are adrift, or in which we bathe while being one with the
embarkation.

That we are suddenly capable of feeling anew the caress of
the wind on our cheeks already suggests that we see it filling the
sail and we again discover the embarkation in its ship's quality
and its particular identity as a cutter or a schooner. That we are
suddenly capable of feeling, anew, in our hair the play of the
wind in which are frolicking birds "*drunken / to be among the
foam unbeknownst to the heavens*," and we shall precisely have
found the sea as sea, again, as what carries the vessel and as
what espouses the sky at the horizon. Through the whiteness of
the sail—swelled by the same wind that plays in our hair and
caresses our cheek—is presented to us "the paper void that its
whiteness protects" and, thanks to this void, "*the desert-like
brightness of the lamp.*" Through this returns to us the color of
"*old gardens reflected by eyes*" and already comes forth "*the young
woman nursing her child.*" Then, we will no longer be "*Lost,
lacking masts and fertile islets*" but, having found the sails again,

we will have found the masts and the ship itself and, through this, the sea that carries it back to the earth. Then we will have again found the world, where we are alongside of things, and nausea will fade like that which was properly nothing.[28]

But in nausea we are strictly incapable of *feeling*[29] this way, because we are drifting shoreless or, more precisely, because we have lost the shore, we are de-rived—because we find ourselves in the absence of any shore, far from any ground. Or, inversely, *because the totality of what is has, on its side, de-rived or lost the shore*. We have our nausea in the specific form of "seasickness," *weil wir schweben*, because we float, suspended,[30] in the drift of the earth, the retreat of the sea, and the disappearance of the vessel itself. Nausea must therefore be understood as the feeling of our being when at sea, such that in the loss of earth's shores and the disappearance of the vessel, the sea itself draws back as sea, and we remain alone, floating in the pure element. Then *es ist einem unheimlich* (WM 32/51/58), which we could translate in at least three ways: then "a *malaise* takes hold of us;"[31] then "we feel oppressed;"[32] then "we are disoriented [*on est dé-paysé*]."[33] Experienced positively as an oppressing *malaise*, this dis-orientation [*dé-paysement*] is born from the recoil of beings in all their aspects (in our example, a drifting away of the earth, the retreat of the sea, and disappearance of the vessel); this recoil holds us at a standstill and in suspense, while no support remains to us, while "there neither remains for nor comes to us—in the drift of beings—anything but this 'none.'" In that sense, nausea "manifests the nothing, *offenbart das Nichts*" (WM 32/51/57).

In Levinas's analysis, three traits of nausea are clearly set forth. In its phenomenon, nausea is not reducible to the determinacy of the object that caused it; nausea lays bare the essential solitude of the being-there it strikes, and manifests noth-

<!-- margin note: 3 Traits of Nausea -->

ingness [*le rien*]. These are, as we know, the distinctive traits of anxiety. And yet, just as anxiety "differs fundamentally from fear" (WM 31/51/57), nausea also differs fundamentally from anxiety. This can be specified, immediately, in the following manner. [Anxiety and nausea differ fundamentally, the one from the other, because in the one and the other case, *we are relating in a fundamentally different way to the nothingness* [*le rien*] *that the one and the other manifest.*[34] In anxiety, the nothing "reveals itself as having a part in the being of the being (*als zugehörig zum Sein des Seienden*)*" (WM 39/51/69), such that it appears as "what makes possible (*die Ermöglichung*) the manifestation of the being as such for human being-there" (WM 35/53/63). The operation of anxiety in its relation to nothing is described, finally, in the following way:

> In the bright night of the nothingness of anxiety, there alone rises up the original opening of the being as such, that means: that it is a being and not nothing. This "and not nothing," added by us in what followed, is not a subsidiary explication, but indeed what makes possible in advance the manifestation of the being in general. The essence of this nothingness, which is our original experience of negation [*du rien originellement néantisant*], lies in that it carries, before all else, the *Dasein* before beings as such. (WM 34/52–53/62)

[Anxiety thus manifests the nothing as being in such a way that it carries us before beings as such and in this way transports us to the heart of the essential knot of being and beings, to the heart of the ontological difference.]

It is precisely in this sense that nausea is fundamentally different from anxiety. In effect, nausea remains somehow set back from the ontological difference, tarrying as it does in the suspense where its appearance [*son phénomène*] set it initially by causing beings in their totality to retreat, thereby manifesting

anxiety & nausea differ in relation to relationship toward nothingness

anxiety

nothingness. However, tarrying in this suspense, nausea re- ⦙
mains at what the analysis of anxiety merely notes before con-
tinuing to pursue its own path. We must return to this analysis
one last time to read the few lines—hearing "nausea" each time
we read "anxiety"—which we have paraphrased above.

In anxiety—we said—"a *malaise* takes hold of us" (*es ist einem unheimlich*; literally: it is uncanny to us). What do the "a" (*es*, or "it")
and the "we" (*einem* or "to one") mean? We cannot say before what
a *malaise* takes hold of us. It takes hold, or comes over us, in general (*Im Ganzen ist einem so*). Everything, and we ourselves, sink
into indifference. Nevertheless, this is not in the sense of a simple
disappearing. On the contrary, in their recoil as such, things turn
toward us. This recoil of the being in its entirety, which invests us
in anxiety, oppresses us. No support remains to us. There neither
remains for nor comes to us—in the drift of beings—anything
but this "none" (*Es bleibt nur und kommt über uns . . . dieses
"kein"*).

In that sense, nausea "manifests the nothing" (WM 32/67/57).
Nausea differs fundamentally from anxiety in that, halted in
the suspense in which it tarries, *nausea becomes the passion of the
return, in the form of the "none," of the* kein, *of this nothing it has
manifested.*
    In its initial moment, our analysis showed that nausea im-
printed a distance upon beings to leave us alone in nothingness; now nausea finds its originality, its essential positive char-
acterization in being this passion of the return of nothing, the
passion of this *über-uns-kommen*, of this coming-over-us or of
this return of the nothing that it manifested. There are not,
nonetheless, two moments in the phenomenon of nausea; simultaneously it reveals nothingness and suffers its return. Only
the necessities of an analysis that sought to show the ontological range of nausea and make its proximity to anxiety luminous

have led us to introduce this duality. We must nevertheless insist upon the fact that, in its phenomenon, nausea is *from the
outset* the passion of the return of nothing or that it is, in other
words, the manifestation of nothingness *as a return*. We henceforth have access to Levinas's description of it, which will allow
us to specify the manner of this return of nothingness. "The
state of nausea that precedes vomiting, and from which vomiting delivers us, encloses us on all sides. Yet it does not come
from outside to confine us. We are revolted from the inside; our
depths smother beneath ourselves; our innards "heave" [*nous
avons "mal au cœur"*] (66; our emphasis)." But what is *revolting*
(66) there, in this presence of ourselves to ourselves, coming to
pass in the form of smothering, could not be brought back to
the situation of the obstacle, whose condition is precisely to *ob-
stare* [to with-stand] and thence to present itself as an *ob-ject* or
Gegen-stand. Beings alone can present themselves as objects and
thus eventually in the manner of an obstacle, while here, and as
we just saw, nausea has "in advance" caused beings in their totality to recoil, to let the nothing or the naught-ing appear, that
is, being as distinct from beings. All the same, this mode of
presence could not also be assimilated in advance to the unfolding of being or *An-wesen* in which being comes to us and
the present (*Gegenwart*) is given as that which comes to tarry
with us (*uns entgegenweilt*).[35] The presence, which comes to
light through nausea, finds its sui generis modality in *adhering
to us*. An adherence without the adhesion of him to whom it
adheres; a horrible adherence, which is translated positively by a
"refusal to remain there, an effort to get out" (66). But this is an
effort "always already characterized as desperate," not only "for
any attempt to act or to think" but in an absolute way, as long
as nausea is "considered in the instant in which it is lived," a requirement we have attempted to maintain from the beginning.

And this despair, this fact of being riveted, constitutes all the anxiety of nausea. In nausea—which amounts to an impossibility of being what one is—we are at the same time riveted to ourselves, enclosed in a tight circle that smothers. We are there, and there is nothing more to be done, nor anything to add to the fact that we have been entirely delivered up, that everything is consumed: *this is the very experience of pure being,* which we have promised from the beginning of this work. (67)

How is it with this "experience of pure being"? Or, to put it otherwise, how must this return of nothing be described? It is while he focuses more closely upon the notion, to set it apart from an ontic interpretation, that Levinas responds to this double question.

But is nausea not a fact of consciousness, which the I knows as one of its states? Is this *existence* itself, or only an *existent*? In so asking, we forget the sui generis implication that constitutes nausea, which allows us to see in it the fulfillment of the very being of the entity that we are [*l'accomplissement de l'être même de l'étant que nous sommes*]. For what constitutes the relationship between nausea and us is nausea itself. The binding, or irremissible, quality of nausea constitutes its very ground. Despair over this ineluctable presence constitutes the presence itself. Thereby, nausea posits itself not only as something absolute, but *as the very act of self-positing: it is the affirmation itself of being.* (68; our emphasis)

Nausea and anxiety differ fundamentally in the manner that each one has of relating to the nothing that they each manifest, or again, in the manner each one has of making it appear. Anxiety, as we have seen, discloses the nothing as that which refers to the being of beings (*als zugehörig zum Sein des Seienden*) and thereby leads us before beings as such. Withdrawn from this operation, nausea manifests the nothing as being itself and manifests being as the very act of positing itself, as the pure act of affirming itself. Nausea manifests the nothing as the pure *fact of being*, which we have considered since the beginning of this introduction. What is the meaning of the nothing, we must ask ourselves, taking up the question posed and ceaselessly rejoined in Heidegger's seminar of 1929? The nothing, outside of any ontical positing or any presentification, appears as being itself and, more precisely, as the very energy of being, as its verb or its verbality, as its *esse*. This amounts to being—which imposes itself beyond any negation and to the point of the supreme negation, that is, the disappearance of any beings posited. Being—which poses and imposes itself to the point of nausea and which, precisely for that reason, nausea is apt to manifest in the recoil it has imprinted in advance upon all beings. What nausea manifests, ultimately, is being as the *there is* [*il y a*] of the *there is being* [*il y a de l'être*], when there is nothing yet [*quand il n'y a pas encore*] or when there is no longer anything because nausea and anxiety have let all that is drift away. What nausea manifests is finally the *there is* [*il y a*] that murmurs at the depths of nothingness itself.

At the end of these analyses, a formula gives itself to or imposes itself on reflection, one that will nevertheless not gain the dignity of a title, in Levinas, before another decade has elapsed from the publication of his essay on escape: the *there is* [*il y a*]. A *there is* of which, still later on, Levinas will write: "It does not exist by virtue of a play on words. The *negation* of all qualifiable things allows the *resurgence* of the impersonal *there is* which, behind every negation, *returns* intact and indifferent to the degree of that negation."[36] In this way, Levinas underscores that dimension of a *return* and of a return *of nothing* that marks the *there is* as it marked being whose meaning was made explicit on the basis of the *Stimmung* (mood, tonality) of nausea. This is a

dimension that is equally the mark of all his analyses of the
there is, published in the immediate postwar period. "Let us
imagine all beings, things, and persons reverting to nothing,"[37]
as we read at the beginning of the chapter "Existence without
Existents," to which the analysis of the *there is* is led in *Existence
and Existents.* And if we attempt in this way to feign the disappearance of every being,[38] what we shall come to describe is
this:

When the forms of things are dissolved in the night, the darkness
of the night, which is neither an object nor the quality of an object, invades like a presence. In the night, where we are riveted to
this darkness, we have nothing to do with anything [*n'avons affaire
à rien*]. But this nothing [*ce rien*] is not that of a pure nothingness
[*d'un pur néant*]. There is no more *this*, nor *that*; there is not
"something." But this universal absence is, in its turn, a presence,
an absolutely unavoidable presence.[39]

And here we have a text, virtually contemporaneous, yet, if
possible, still more explicit:

There remains after this imaginary destruction of all things, not
something, but the fact that *there is*. The absence of all things returns like a presence: like the site wherein everything has sunken,
like an atmospheric density, like a plenitude of emptiness or like
the murmur of silence. There is, after this destruction of things
and beings, the "field of forces" of existing, impersonal. Something that is neither a subject, nor a substantive. The fact of existing, which imposes itself when there is nothing more. And it is
anonymous: there is no one and nothing that might take this existence upon itself. It is impersonal like "it is raining" or "it is
hot." An existing that returns, whatever be the negation by which
one sets it aside. This is something like a pure existing that cannot
be remitted.[40]

We therefore see now that, in the essay on escape, what gets designed by the name of "pure being," or being qua being, or the fact of being or of the existence of what is is already very precisely that which will later on be thought as the *there is*: the return of nothing into an unalterably binding presence. We will leave it to the reader to refer to the passages noted if he desires the details of the analysis. Here, we would like to limit ourselves to three remarks. It is not without interest to note, first, that Blanchot sees in the *there is* "one of Levinas's most fascinating propositions."[41] Indeed, when Blanchot attempts to think what he designates as the Outside, or the other night—concepts that later break through into the words "neuter" and "disaster" but which, in some places, can only be *thought* in relation to the *there is*[42]—matches Levinas's analyses quite precisely, at the level of their form. Thus, we read in *L'espace littéraire*:

In the night, everything has disappeared. This is the first night. . . . But when everything has disappeared in the night, "the everything has disappeared" appears. This is the *other* night. Night is this apparition of the "everything has disappeared." It is what we sense in advance when dreams replace sleep, when the dead pass into the deep of the night, when night's depth appears in those who have disappeared. Apparitions, phantoms, and dreams are an allusion to this empty night. . . . What appears in the night is the night that appears, and this strangeness comes not only from something invisible, which might reveal itself under cover of dark and at the shadows' summons. Here the invisible is what one cannot cease to see; it is the incessant making itself seen.[43]

In Blanchot's language, that which makes all the weight and all the horror of being, understood in the neuter or as the *there is*, breaks through in a startling way, as does all the passivity of the being-there or *Dasein* upon whom an utterly obligatory pres-

ence is imposed, one which being-there undergoes without being able to take it in charge.

We should note next that the concept of being Levinas develops in his first reflections will be maintained without change
into his most mature work. In *Otherwise than Being or Beyond
Essence*, as well as in *Totality and Infinity*, though we do not find
the explicit analysis of the notion of the *there is*, this is only because his use of it is accompanied by a reference to *Existence
and Existents*. Yet nothing would be more false than to suppose
that this notion itself is forgotten or relegated to the background. To those who supposed as much, the highly interesting
preface to the second edition of *Existence and Existents* (from
1978) brings a flagrant denial of this supposition. "The notion
of the *there is*, developed in this book, now thirty years old,
seems to us the best part," as the first sentence notes. Further
on, indicating "those elements in these early developments to
which I still attach a certain importance today," Levinas writes:
"These are the places in the texts of the first part where I venture a phenomenology of laziness, fatigue, effort, [as well as] of
the traits marked by the desert-like character, obsessive and
horrible, of *being*, understood according to the *there is*; but it is
above all the description of this *there is* itself, and the insistence
on its inhuman neutrality."[44] In fact, one might say that in
Otherwise than Being or Beyond Essence—where the stratagem
of the feint is, moreover, abandoned[45]—the *there is* truly acquires the status of a key notion in becoming explicitly synonymous with *essence*, exactly designating the manner of being
or what many of the book's pages authorize us to call, in this
sense, its *esse*.[46] Essence is the only notion that will be the object of an explicit, preliminary note in the book: "The domi-
nant note, necessary to understanding this discourse and even
its title, must be emphasized at the beginning of this book,

though it will be frequently repeated at the heart of the work: the term *essence* here expresses *being* different from *beings*, the German *Sein* distinguished from *Seiendes*, the Latin *esse* distinguished from the Scholastic *ens*."[47] Essence is thus emphasized, despite a reticence in the book. "We have not dared to write *essance* as the history of language would require, in which the suffix *-ance*, deriving from *-antia* or *-entia*, gave birth to abstract nouns of action."[48] Nevertheless, this notion will come to be written "*essance*" in the publications immediately following, thereby justifying its necessity: "We are writing *essance* with an *a* to designate with this word the verbal sense of the word *being* [*être*]: the effectuation of being, the *Sein* distinct from the *Seiendes*."[49] Thus, in *Otherwise than Being or Beyond Essence*, where Levinas expressed his most mature and nuanced thought, the very mode of being's effectuation, the very *esse* of this *essance* leads back to the *there is* or to the absorption in this pure *fact of being* that *On Escape* proposed.

The imperturbable essence, equal and indifferent to any responsibility that it henceforth encompasses, turns, as in insomnia, from this neutrality and equality into monotony, anonymity, insignificance, into an incessant buzzing that nothing can stop any longer, and which absorbs all signification, even that of which this bustling about is a modality. Essence stretching on indefinitely, without reserve, without possible interruption—the equality of essence not justifying, in all fairness, any instant's halt, without respite, without any possible suspension—this is the horrifying *there is* behind any finality proper to the thematizing *ego*, which cannot fail to sink into the essence it thematizes.[50]

It is this way because essence, or being as different from beings, is given in fact as the difference between the two. It is given as the ontological difference, and this difference is interpreted as the "amphibology of being and beings,"[51] as an insoluble equivocation where being qua verb [*l'être-verbe*] "turns into a noun," while being qua noun is "verbalized." As an articulation of presence and of the present, essence will thus take place as an interminable presence, stretching out indefinitely and coming back to fill any void that could be inscribed, through negation, not in presence but rather in the being itself, in the present. It is in this way that essence will be reabsorbed in the *there is*.

My final remark starts from a statement of fact and a certain astonishment. All this meditation on being riveted and on the escape whose need it elicits is also a meditation on the body, and all the phenomena the meditation analyzes—need, malaise, shame-filled nudity, nausea—are phenomena tied to the body. And yet, the word "body" is scarcely present in the text; it is pronounced only in passing (at six points, I would venture to say, in two groups of three occurrences, which each time are but a single one, and two times in relation to shame). One year before "On Escape," Levinas had nevertheless published an essay that was intentional and effectively philosophical, but which also responded to the most pressing historical concerns: "Reflections on Hitlerism."[52]

Now, this essay, in many respects foreshadowing "On Escape," thematized the body explicitly as the site of a sui generis bind. More precisely, his intent was to set forth what was specifically new in the phenomenon of Hitler, and he concluded in a radical way. "It is not this or that dogma of democracy, of parliamentarianism, of a dictatorial regime; nor is a religious politics what is in question. It is the very humanity of man."[53] In the form in which it could be grasped in 1934 (the date is worth our noting), Hitlerism was a challenge because it questioned the idea of the freedom of mind that liberalism had inherited from the common fund of Judeo-Christianity. To be

sure, Marxism had already attacked this conception by subject-
ing consciousness to its conditions of existence. Nevertheless:
"To become aware of one's social situation is for Marx himself
to free oneself from the fatalism that situation contains. *A conception truly opposed to the European notion of man would be possible only if the situation to which he is* riveted *did not add itself
to him, but instead made up the very ground of his being. This is
the paradoxical demand that the experience of our* body *seems to
realize.*"[54]

Still, we should not hold the body as an obstacle and consider it fundamentally foreign. We must surpass the classical
conception of the body and on the basis, for example, of the
phenomenon of pain ("called, lightly, physical"),[55] put our fin-
ger on the *adherence* of body to the Ego—for against pain the
revolt of the spirit and its refusal to remain with the body
proves henceforth desperate. "The body is not only a happy or
unhappy accident putting us in relation to the implacable
world of matter, *its adherence to the Ego has its own value.* The
adherence from which *we do not escape* and which no metaphor
could confuse with the presence of an external object. It is a
union whose tragic taste of the definitive could not be altered
by anything."[56] We thus see clearly that the body is thought
here according to concepts that, one year later, will be used in
"On Escape."

Nonetheless, it is one thing to recognize this tragic sui
generis as tied to the existence of the body as such, but another
thing to found a society upon a determination of man that is
satisfied to raise this, or even lay claim to the body, as supreme
value.

The importance attributed to this feeling of the body, with which
the western spirit never wanted to be satisfied, is at the base of a

new conception of man. The biological, with all the fatality it contains, becomes more than an *object* of spiritual life, it becomes its heart. The mysterious voices of the blood, the appeals of heredity and of the past, for which the body serves as an enigmatic vehicle, lose their nature as problems subject to a solution by a sovereign, free Ego. The Ego brings only the unknown variables of these problems to their resolution. It is made up of them. The essence of humanity is no longer in freedom but in a kind of bondage. To be truly oneself is not to take flight over contingencies ever foreign to the freedom of the Ego, it is on the contrary to become aware of the ineluctable bondage unique to your body. It is especially to accept this bondage. . . . A society based on consanguinity flows immediately from this concretization of the spirit. And then, if race did not exist, it would be necessary to invent it![57]

There is, therefore, an intrinsically particularistic character to a society founded, like the Hitlerist one, upon this understanding of, or claim to, the body as the site of adherence. In 1935, Levinas prophetically drew this consequence: "How is universality comparable with racism? There is in racism—and this is in the logic of its primary inspiration—a fundamental modification of the very idea of universality. *It must give way to the idea of expansion*, for the expansion of a force presents an entirely different structure than that of the propagation of an idea."

In fact, this expansion "brings at the same time its own form of universalization: war, conquest."[58] In the year that followed, Hitler's seizure of power and the unleashing of World War II were foreseeable, not to the gaze of the historian, but to that of the philosopher. Yet perhaps something else was also foreseeable: the evolution of racist anti-Semitism toward the "Final Solution." It is, in effect, perfectly coherent with Levinas's analyses that paragraph four of the Nazi Party's program stated that "only he who is of German blood, independently of his confession, can be a compatriot [*Volksgenosse*]. A Jew cannot be a compatriot."[59] Thus was created a category of non-"compatriots" and, consequently, of noncitizens. Thus was created a category of "others," of whom it was going to be necessary to purify Germany, then Europe. But that this purification should finally take the form of *extermination* was perhaps inscribed in the racist conception—notably, the biologistic conception—of man within Hitlerism. In effect, with this conception, "chained to his body, man finds himself denied the power to escape from himself."[60]

Yet to the man who is designated as "other" and who, as such, is the racial enemy of the human species, there was left no exit to escape the vengeance of the gaze thus focused on him—not even conversion sufficed, which had always served as an escape route over the centuries of Christian anti-Semitism. It is, necessarily, in that body to which he is riveted—and from which he could, for this reason, never escape—that he is pursued. We may thus wonder whether such a design did not carry the seeds of an extermination, in the exclusively physical sense of the term. This observation is not purely retrospective; it founds its probability on the philosophical reflections of 1934, clarified by the meditation of 1935. Moreover, it finds its necessity in a decisive remark by Raul Hilberg, who stands between the intentionalists and the functionalists in this debate: "In the early days of 1933, when the first functionary wrote down the first definition of 'non-Aryan' in an administrative order, the fate of the European Jewry was sealed."[61]

2. From Escape to Otherwise than Being

The remarks in the first part of this introduction were to allow us to comprehend the signification of the word *being* in Levinas's 1935 study and, more precisely, to show how being was thought, there, as *there is*, even though this particular name had not yet been given to being. This preoccupation led us to read alongside Levinas's analyses, to cross them at certain points, without following the how of their procedure. This is an externalist prejudice that always carries within it the threat of violence, but which alone (this is one of the theses of our approach) lets us bring to light what is in question in a text. A position that could only be upheld insofar as it shows its validity; it should be abandoned as soon as maintaining it carries the risk of making us lose whole levels of the analysis or, more serious still, the original notion that the analysis was attempting to present. Let us turn then to this notion of "escape," which up to now our analysis has avoided addressing—just as it avoided the relevant passages from Levinas's text—since this notion gave the essay its title and constitutes its "inimitable theme" (54). It is necessary "to rechart our trajectory" here, but it will be all the easier to perform in that it consists in fact in prolonging analyses we had foreshortened toward the essential end of clarity in our exposition.

Let us take up the question again where we left it.

The very fact of existing refers only to itself [*à soi*]. It is that through which all powers and all properties are posited. *The escape we envisage should appear to us like the inner structure of this fact of self-positing.* We will attempt to discover escape in a state of affairs where the fact of self-positing [*se poser*] is laid bare, freed from any consideration of natures, qualities, or powers that are posited and that mask the event through which they *are*. (56–57; our emphasis, except the last word)

We know, presently, that it is through nausea, in which the existent is submerged by its existence, where it glimpses itself chained to being inasmuch as it is riveted to its own being, that being is imposed like the fact of being or like the pure fact of imposition, in immobility, to the point of nausea. In prolonging this analysis, then, we shall be able to approach the notion of escape.

At the end of our attempt to explicate the *Stimmung* (mood, tonality) of nausea, we had read this: "In nausea—which amounts to an impossibility of being what one is—we are at the same time riveted to ourselves, enclosed in a tight circle that smothers. We are there, and there is nothing more to be done, or anything to add to this fact that we have been entirely delivered up, that everything is consumed: *this is the very experience of pure being*, which we have promised from the beginning of this work" (66–67). We must now read the lines that follow: "However, this 'nothing-more-to-be-done' is the mark of a limit-situation in which the uselessness of any action is precisely the sign of the supreme instant from which we can only depart. The experience of pure being is at the same time the experience of its internal antagonism and of the escape that foists itself on us" (67). The experience of escape is one with "the experience of pure being" insofar as it is simultaneously the imperious necessity and the rigorous impossibility of getting out. It is an imperious necessity because "the experience of pure being" shows itself as the experience of "the horror . . . of being as such" (53); it is a strict impossibility if nausea is grasped, as it must be and as we have attempted to do, "in the instant in which it is lived and in the atmosphere that surrounds it" (66).

Under this aspect, again, nausea must be thought in its diver-
gent proximity to anxiety, which "takes away our words" and in
which "is silenced every saying that says 'is' (*schweigt . . . jedes
'Ist'-sagen*)" (WM 32/51/59). In the instant in which it is experienced, nausea—deprived of words, the pure passion of the
nothing's return, which encloses and embraces it—has the possibility neither of thinking nor of thinking itself [*penser ni de se
penser*], nor therefore of attending to an exit for itself; nausea is
experienced simply as the pure need for a pure escape, that is,
an escape that its essential indetermination characterizes in the
first place. Nausea, which does not *know* even whether vomiting will come to deliver it, *cannot* represent a way out to itself.
Deprived of words, cheated out of any use of the "little words
'it is,'" it is just as much *time* that will permit it to give itself a
future and to exercise the reflection of which it is deprived. In
this way, its essential proximity to suffering shows itself, just as
Blanchot thought. "Suffering is suffering," the latter writes,
"when one can no longer suffer it, and when, because of this
non-power, one cannot cease suffering it. A singular situation.
Time is as though arrested, merged with its interval. . . . What
has happened? Suffering has simply lost its hold on time, and
has made us lose time."[62] But if this is how it is, then to nausea
is refused the sole way out that could be offered to it: death,
which *Time and the Other* determined as "never now" and thus
as "eternal future."[63] Let us use this remark to specify that what
comes to light here is the present, which is also that to which
nausea attaches itself, like suffering as well. Nevertheless, this is
in no way the now (*jetzt*, *vûv*, or *nunc*) of the metaphysics of
presence, but something like *time refused*, and this a present deprived of its most felicitous possibility: to be "the apogee of
time and the condition of freedom," as we read in note 9 in this
text. But let us return to death, or rather to its phantom.

"Death is not the exit toward which escape thrusts us. Death can only appear to it if escape reflects upon itself. As such, nausea discovers only the nakedness of being in its plenitude and in its utterly binding presence" (67).

What escape would have as its task to untie—were it able to do so—is what came to light in the analysis of shame; a shame that is, moreover, one with nausea. We leapt over this stage in Levinas's reflection to come directly to nausea; we must presently return to the earlier stage.

Shame: If shame is present, it means that we cannot hide what we should like to hide. The necessity of fleeing, of hiding oneself, is put in check by the impossibility of fleeing *oneself*. What appears in shame is thus precisely the fact of being *riveted to oneself*, the radical impossibility of fleeing *oneself* to hide from *oneself*, the unalterably *binding presence of the I to itself* [*du moi à soi-même*].[64] Nakedness is shameful when it is the *sheer visibility* [*patence*] *of our being*, of its ultimate intimacy. And the nakedness of our body is not that of a material thing, antithesis of spirit, but the nakedness of our total being in all its fullness and solidity, of its most brutal expression, of which we could not fail to take note. . . . It is therefore our intimacy, that is, *our presence to ourselves*, that is shameful. It reveals not our nothingness but rather the totality of our existence. Nakedness is the need to excuse one's existence. Shame is, in the last analysis, an existence that seeks excuses. What shame discovers [*découvre*] is the being who *uncovers* himself [*se* découvre]. (64–65; emphasis added except for the last word)[65]

We now see precisely that escape would in fact have, as task, to untie the essential link between the existent and its existence, of which nausea has shown us all its depth and obligation; we see that the task of escaping would be "*to break that most radical and unalterably binding of chains, the fact that the I* [moi] *is oneself* [soi-même]" (55).

These specifications brought to the notion of escape explain the insistence with which Levinas, at the beginning of the text, attempts to set the verb "to get out" [*sortir*] apart from anything that could dull its sharpness in orienting it according to some transitivity. "It is this category of getting out, inassimilable neither to renovation nor to creation, which we must grasp in all its purity" (54; see esp. pp. 49–56). But these remarks also place us under the obligation to ask ourselves *how* we might perform such a disengagement, such a disintrication or a getting-out [*sortie*], when considered in their purity. And it will not fail to be obvious that the definition of the "how" is precisely what is lacking in Levinas's 1935 study. It is not, however, that the question was set aside or omitted; only that the sole modality envisioned for untightening the vise, namely pleasure, proves to be incapable of accomplishing what it ought to have permitted and seemed to promise. It is therefore extremely important to see in what way pleasure is the carrier of a promise of escaping or of getting-out, and in what way escape ultimately shows itself to be fallacious or disappointing. It is worthwhile to describe pleasure's mode of being [*la façon du plaisir*].

Pleasure appears as it develops. It is neither there as a whole, nor does it happen all at once. And furthermore, it will never be whole or integral. Progressive movement is a characteristic trait of this phenomenon, which is by no means a simple state. This is a movement that does not tend toward a goal, for it has no end. It exists wholly in the enlargement of its own amplitude, which is like the rarefaction of our existence [*être*], or its swooning. In the very depths of incipient pleasure there opens something like abysses, ever deeper, into which our existence, no longer resisting, hurls itself. There is something dizzying to pleasure's unfolding [*devenir*]. There is ease or cowardice. The [human] being feels its substance somehow draining from it; it grows lighter, as if drunk, and disperses. . . . We therefore note in pleasure an abandonment, a loss of oneself, a getting out of oneself, an ecstasy: so many traits that describe the promise of escape contained in pleasure's essence. (61)

But for all that, the promise contained in pleasure is fallacious, the escape that it lets us glimpse "is a deceptive escape" (62). What is inscribed, moreover, in its very becoming, in this *progression* that it *is*, is deception. For pleasure does not go toward an end, it goes rather toward a crest or a summit, toward an orgasm in some sense, toward "the supreme breaking where the being believes [*croit*] in complete ecstasy"—but which forms a unity with "the moment where the pleasure breaks up," which itself was united with the moment in which the being who had believed in its liberation "is entirely disappointed and ashamed to find himself again existing" (61).

One might almost say that pleasure could only actualize escape in the eroticism of a praying mantis and understand, more seriously, on the basis of these descriptions, that the latent presence of death in all erotic art has nothing accidental about it. To come back to our text, we must now see how pleasure is "an escape that fails."

If, like a process that is far from closing up on itself, pleasure appears in a constant surpassing of oneself, it breaks just at the moment where it seems to get out absolutely. It develops with an increase in promises, which become richer the closer it comes to its paroxysm, but these promises are never kept. . . . In itself, on a strictly affective level, pleasure is disappointment and deceit [*deception et tromperie*]. It is not disappointment through the role it plays in life, or through its destructive effects, or even through its moral indignity, but rather through its internal unfolding. . . . And at the moment of its disappointment, which should have been that of its triumph, the meaning of its failure is underscored by shame. (62–63)

As nausea's companion, shame is, as we have seen, the shameful and already in some sense nauseated trial of our presence to ourselves in the nudity of our bodies, and we are therefore obliged to note that pleasure leads just as precisely to the contrary of what it promised, as does absolute freedom when it turns into terror.

What, ultimately, shall we make of this notion of escape, which is so abstract that it does not succeed in getting past the appearance [*allure*] of a pure demand and turns into its contrary the moment it seems apt to be concretized? We must admit, and emphasize, here that the 1936 writing does not go beyond the position of this pure need to get out, which it simply attempts to present in all its purity. Should we then speak of a failure? And should we not agree that this failure is the price to pay for having wanted to philosophize about a chimera? Is it not the price to pay for having wanted to make his own a thematic that was, no doubt, "inimitable"? Is this not all the more so, that this thematic is also the most perfect of absurdities: the project of "getting out of being"? And, more precisely, according to what we have been allowed to understand, it is to get out otherwise than by death, otherwise than toward nothingness; it is to get out of being, understood in its verbal sense. Is this failure not the ransom of a mad thinking that wanted to defy the laws of logic to think, not a third term but, between being and nothingness, an excluded middle [*un tiers-exclu*]?

And yet the essay on escape finds an ancestor in idealism for its inimitable thematic. This is an ancestor at once highly respectable in its aspirations and impotent in its realizations.

Highly respectable in that "in its initial inspiration" it "aims to surpass being"—impotent because it "modifies the structure of the existent but does not tackle its existence" (72). The adventure of idealism consequently merits being described in the following manner.

IDEALISM: The emancipation of idealism in regard to being is based upon its undervaluation. Consequently, at the very moment when idealism imagines it has surpassed being, it is invaded by being from all sides. Those intellectual relations into which idealism dissolved the universe are no less its existences—neither inert nor opaque, to be sure—and they do not escape the laws of being. Idealism is exposed not only to the attacks of all who charge it with sacrificing sensuous reality and with ignoring or scorning the concrete and poignant demands of human beings prey to their everyday problems. Consequently, idealism is charged with being unable to command and to guide. But it does not even have the excuse of escaping from being. Indeed, at the level to which it leads us, idealism finds being—in a subtler form, and one that beckons us to a false serenity—always the same, having relinquished none of its characteristics (72–73).

This is the tragedy of idealism, which becomes transparent when it becomes transcendental. Then thinking fixes its task as "surpassing being [*dépasser l'être*]," which it thinks about as beings in totality [*étant en totalité*], as the set of objects of experience, toward the conditions of their possibility. But then, thinking returns just as much from beings [*de l'étant*] toward their *being* [*vers son* être], though it may not itself realize this—as we can show when we think idealism's work from a site where thinking distinguishes between being and beings.

This tragedy, if we may call it that, of idealism in fact reveals in an essential manner the deep movement that governs what, in his later years, Levinas would call "the philosophy handed down to us," in regard to which the project of an "escape" aiming to "get out of being" can only appear as an absurdity. The text attests that Levinas grasped this clearly from 1935 on.

And yet progress has not brought Western philosophy to surpass being entirely. When it discovered, beyond things, the realms of the ideal, of consciousness, and of becoming—our first model of being—it was incapable of denying these realms an existence, since the benefit of its discovery consisted precisely in making them be. Ontologism in its broadest meaning remained the fundamental dogma of all thought. Despite all its subtlety, it remained prisoner of an elementary and simple principle, according to which one could think and feel only that which exists or is supposed to exist. A principle more imperious than that of non-contradiction, since here nothingness itself—to the degree that thinking encounters it—gets clothed with existence, and so we must without restriction state, against Parmenides, that non-being is (p. 71).[66]

Yet the impotence of idealism—or its tragedy—must nevertheless not mask its respectability and its fecundity for a more audacious thought that could "measure without fear all the weight of being and its universality. It is the path where we recognize the inanity of acts and thoughts incapable of taking the place of an event that breaks up existence in the very accomplishment of its existence. Such deeds and thoughts must not conceal from us, then, the originality of escape" (73). The task incumbent upon thinking is to fulfill, in some sense, the program of idealism, to complete the work that it cannot realize, though it be its own. When this is understood, we must again insist upon the fact that Levinas's thought, here, does not get beyond its programmatic character, as is underscored by the very expression of the sentence that closes the essay: "It is a matter of getting out of being by a new path, at the risk of overturning certain notions that to common sense and the wisdom of the nations seemed the most evident" (73). What we are not told, then, is what this "new path" could be.

It was going to be the task, however, of the entire coming work, which we glimpse herein "through the magic crystal," to attempt to trace this path or to fulfill this program. The notion of escape was thus pregnant with a future as rich as the concept of being elaborated through it—with one difference, however, and of extreme importance: whereas, as we have seen at the end of the preceding section, being, understood as neutral or as *there is*, was going to maintain its resonance without alteration until the most mature works, the notion of escape was going to be purely and simply abandoned as such. Yet the abandonment was nevertheless extremely fecund, since it was to give rise to successive metamorphoses of the abandoned notion; and this, in such a way that to retrace their unfolding would also be to retrace the very evolution of Levinas's work. That amounts to saying that here we shall only be able to sketch out the essential traits of this evolution, without discussing them in any way and without even describing them in an exhaustive and thereby satisfying fashion.

Escape will find its first metamorphosis, in *Existence and Existents* and its contemporary lectures on *Time and the Other*, thanks to the *hypostasis*, "where being, stronger than negation, is subject as it were to beings, and existence to the existent."[67] The hypostasis amounts to the position of a subject within being, which, just like the *there is*, submerges it. The hypostasis thereby supposes an inversion in the relationship between existence and the existent. Now, in the "imaginary" situation of the *there is* or in the trial of nausea such as we described it, the existent was entirely subservient to the existence that overflowed it from all sides, enclosed it from everywhere, and raised or heaved it up from the inside, while it became in some sense "the object rather than the subject of an anonymous thought."[68] In the case of the hypostasis, the existent "bears its existing [*exister*] like an attribute, it is master of this existing as the subject is master of its attribute."[69] The hypostasis's primary condition is found in the possibility of sleeping and, thanks to its sleep, of liberating itself from the oppressive presence of the nothing that becomes insomnia. In this way, it is to be thought of as a metamorphosis of escape, and it is interesting to note that the hypostasis is designated elsewhere as "an *escape into self* [*une évasion en soi*]."[70] Escaping into oneself, as the constitution of a subject or an I [*Moi*] liable thus to escape, will be the problematic of *Totality and Infinity*. At the level of this work, however, this "deliverance from the horror of the *there is* is evinced in the contentment of enjoyment [*jouissance*]."[71] We can therefore read these few sentences, whose thorough understanding presupposes, nevertheless, a reading of the second section of *Totality and Infinity*.[72] "One becomes a subject of being not by assuming being but in enjoying happiness, by the internalization of enjoyment, which is also an exaltation, an 'above being'. . . . To be I [*Moi*] is to exist in such a way as to be already beyond being, in happiness."[73]

For all that, this figure of escape is not yet suitable for the "inimitable thematic that proposes we get out of, or beyond, being," which the 1935 study had promised. Even though its ambition is infinitely more exalted, even though its intention is entirely different, Levinas's thinking in *Totality and Infinity* seems to limit itself "simply to inverting the terms of the famous Heideggerian difference, privileging beings over being,"[74] when its ultimate design—not yet expressed adequately, we must emphasize, in either *Existence and Existents* or in *Totality and Infinity*—is to "allow meanings from *beyond the ontological difference* to signify."[75] An intention that puts radically into question the subjectivity toward which, as we will at least have noted, the preceding metamorphoses of escape were leading. But to this intention the metamorphoses of escape were neither suitable [*convenir*], nor do they suffice insofar as, in positing the human subject as the "being par excellence" and in seeming to privilege the latter in relation to being, "to the detriment of being," they considered the subject as an I [*Moi*] who "has identity as its content" or as "the being for which existing consists in identifying it, in rediscovering its identity throughout all that happens to it"—in a word, whose existence consists in "being the Same, not relatively but absolutely."[76] This is an I [*Moi*] *positing itself* as the Same in the hypostasis, or *making itself* such through enjoyment's own dialectic; an I [*Moi*] securing in this way its deliverance from the horror of the *there is* by mastering its existence. This is not yet, and far from it, "to recognize in subjectivity an ex-ception upsetting the conjunction of *essence*, beings, and the 'difference' ";[77] it is not yet *to see in the human the crisis of being.*[78]

For that, it shall be necessary to think the subject, in itself or in its subjectivity as such, as already "evaded" or "escaped" [*évadé*]—*because already expelled.* For that, it shall no longer suffice to posit the subject as the Same and, as it were, factor or agent of the Same. It shall be necessary to think the subject as the *Other-within-the-Same,* and therefore already as the knot of a dis-quiet that does not let the subject return to itself to posit itself in a stable identity, and therefore already as the site of an expulsion. This amounts to an expulsion by the Other installing itself, to beat within, at the heart of the Same;[79] and it is an expulsion for the Other [*pour l'Autre*], who demands more or farther than the possible and thus indelibly marks identity. For this, it shall be necessary, finally, to write *Otherwise than Being or Beyond Essence*, just as, to understand this, it will be necessary to read it. Without presuming to provide access to this masterwork—which is not the purpose of this introduction—we would like to cite a few lines in which the meanings we just evoked are brought together admirably. "The identity of the *same* in the 'ego' [*je*] comes to it despite itself from the outside, as an election or an inspiration, in the form of the uniqueness of someone assigned. The subject is for the other; its own being passes away [*s'en aller*] for the other; its being dies away, turning into signification."[80] A movement of "swooning" that, by contrast with pleasure and because it knows no orgasm, does not inscribe in its trajectory the break contemporary with ecstasy and the shameful return to its point of departure. This is a movement of detachment or disengagement [*déprise*] without reserve, passive, more passive than the passivity of receptivity, whose essence is precisely to assume again what it receives, passive to the point of being unable to consent to or resist its assignation as a subject elected or accused or cornered into responsibility. It is passive with a passivity that would equal only that of nausea, where the existent is submerged by an existence that it can in no way master. Yet, in the midst of this passivity, there is a subjectivity again dislodged from its torpor, sobered even from its own nausea, awakened from its "hangover" [*"gueule de bois"*]—a subjectivity exposed without any possible defense to the alterity of the Other, who identifies it as a subject by accusing it, or by electing it to die in its place or to *substitute* itself. A subjectivity, in this sense, *structured like escape*, that is, an inversion into the *otherwise than being* of the I [*Moi*] who identifies itself by persevering in its being, by existing to the beat of ess*a*nce.

In this outline of an analysis, two things seem to us to require emphasis. The passivity of subjectivity in the trial of election refers to the passivity of nausea, in which being discloses itself as the pure fact of being and is already profiled as the neutrality of the *there is*. Thus, this notion of the *there is*, which already shows itself as the very manner of ess*a*nce, as we noted above, acquires an eminent function again in the pages of *Otherwise than Being or Beyond Essence*. That is what the pages of the chapter "Sense and the *There Is*" show—pages to our mind essential or truly *central,* in Blanchot's sense of the term.[81] We cite the following lines from them.

The *there is* is all the weight that alterity weighs supported by a subjectivity that does not found it. But one must not say that the *there is* results from a "subjective impression." In this overflowing of sense by non-sense, the sensibility—the Self [*le Soi*]—is first brought out [*s'accuse seulement*], in its bottomless passivity, like a pure sensible point, like dis-interestedness, or like the subversion of essence. Behind the anonymous rustling of the *there is* subjectivity reaches passivity without a taking in charge or assumption. Assumption would already put into correlation with an act this passivity of the *otherwise than being*, this substitution from the inner side of the opposition of active and passive, subjective and objective, being and becoming. In the subjectivity of the *Self,* substitution is passivity's ultimate retraction or withdrawal; this is the opposite of taking in charge, in which is fulfilled—or presupposed—the *receptivity* that describes the finitude of a transcendental *I think*. The identity of the chosen one—that is, the one assigned—which signifies prior to being, should take hold and affirm itself in the *essence* that negativity itself determines. In order to bear without compensation, it requires the excessive or disheartening hubbub [*l'é-cœurant remue-ménage*] and encumberment of the *there is*.[82]

Thus, the horror of the *there is*—of which the analysis of nausea had already measured the weight under other names—itself becomes a *condition* in the intrigue of subjectivity.

On its side, subjectivity may no longer be thought as a

"getting out" of being, but rather, renouncing this dangerously spatial metaphor, is explained as the *deneutralization* of the *there is*.[83] It is no longer named "escape," but *deliverance*, in the intrigue of signification, as is explained in the lines that follow those we just read.

Signification, the for-the-other, will not be an act of free assumption, will not be a *for-itself* that denies its own resignation, nor the playful gratuity in which the gravity of alterity goes up in smoke in the cheerfulness and ecstasy (of him who only conceals himself) as a "nothing at all" in the equivalence of everything and nothing. Signification is the ethical deliverance of the Self [*Soi*] through substitution for the other. It consumes itself as expiation for the other. It is a Self from before any initiative, from before any beginning, signifying anarchically, before any present. The deliverance into itself of an I [*Moi*] awakened from its imperialist dream, its transcendental imperialism, awakened to itself, a patience as subjection to everything.[84]

These lines—which, we repeat, require our reading the entire work to understand them—allow us nevertheless to perceive clearly the meaning of the ultimate metamorphosis of escape: *the ethical de-neutralization of the there is in the intrigue of the otherwise than being*.

In this way the "mad" thought of escape finishes by compelling thought to that other, still "madder"—or more *holy?*— one, of "passing over to being's other, otherwise than being. Not *to be otherwise*, but *otherwise than being*,"[85] where alone this thought takes on its full meaning. In this way, what the first essay allowed us to glimpse in what was still a confused form now finds the means to say itself only by engulfing itself resolutely in non-reason [*dé-raison*], in the outside-the-word [*hors-logos*] that the first essay only suggested: the thought of an excluded middle [*d'un tiers-exclu*]. From one "madness" to the other, through the advances and retreats of a meditation compelled to open its own path by forging its own language,[86] the course of a single reflection is sketched, one devoted to the task of thinking by limiting itself to a single thought.[87] This is a faithfulness that defines what continues to hold the name "philosophy." That it should nevertheless have taken close to forty years and several books—which were not just intermediaries designed to go from one to the other, in order that the last one could keep the promise latent in the first one—allows, in its turn, a second dimension of the work of Levinas's philosophy to appear, one that marks it as the exercise of the longest patience.

Paris, August 1981
Revised, December 1997

ON ESCAPE

Being assaults freed.
~ Mon vs non

I

The revolt of traditional philosophy against the idea of being originates in the discord between human freedom and the
brutal fact of being that assaults this freedom. The conflict
from which the revolt arises opposes man to the world, not
man to himself. The simplicity of the subject lies beyond the
struggles that tear it apart and that, within man, set the "I"
[*moi*] against the "non-I" [*non-moi*]. These struggles do not
break up the unity of the "I," which—when purified of all that
is not authentically human in it—is given to peace with itself,
completes itself, closes on and rests upon itself.

Despite its heroic conception of human destiny, the romanticism of the eighteenth and nineteenth centuries does not
deviate from this ideal of peace. The individual is called upon
to loosen the grasp of the foreign reality [*réalité étrangère*] that
chokes it, but this is in order to assure the full flowering of its

ideal of peace

own reality. Only the struggle with the obstacle is open to the heroism of the individual; this struggle is turned toward the stranger [*l'étranger*]. No one is more proud than Rousseau or Byron; no one is more self-sufficient.

[This conception of the "I" [*moi*] as self-sufficient is one of the essential marks of the bourgeois spirit and its philosophy. As sufficiency for the petit bourgeois, this conception of the "I" nonetheless nourishes the audacious dreams of a restless and enterprising capitalism. This conception presides over capitalism's work ethic, its cult of initiative and discovery, which aims less at reconciling man with himself than at securing for him the unknowns of time and things. The bourgeois admits no inner division [*déchirement intérieur*] and would be ashamed to lack confidence in himself, but he is concerned about reality and the future, for they threaten to break up the uncontested equilibrium of the present where he holds sway [*où il possède*]. He is essentially conservative, but there is a worried conservatism. The bourgeois is concerned with business matters and science as a defense against things and all that is unforeseeable in them. His instinct for possession is an instinct for integration, and his imperialism is a search for security. He would like to cast the white mantle of his "internal peace" over the antagonism that opposes him to the world. His lack of scruples is the shameful form of his tranquil conscience. Yet, prosaically materialistic [*médiocrement matérialiste*], he prefers the certainty of tomorrow to today's enjoyments. He demands guarantees in the present against the future, which introduces unknowns into those solved problems from which he lives. What he possesses becomes capital, carrying interest or insurance against risks, and his future, thus tamed, is integrated in this way with his past.

Yet this category of sufficiency is conceived in the image of *being* such as things offer it to us. They *are*. Their essence and their properties can be imperfect; the very fact of being is placed beyond the distinction between the perfect and the imperfect. The brutality of its assertion [that of the fact of being] is absolutely sufficient and refers to nothing else. Being is: there is nothing to add to this assertion as long as we envision in a being only its existence. This reference to oneself is precisely what one states when one speaks of the identity of being. Identity is not a property of being, and it could not consist in the resemblance between properties that, in themselves, suppose identity. Rather, it expresses the sufficiency of the fact of being, whose absolute and definitive character no one, it seems, could place in doubt.

And Western philosophy, in effect, has never gone beyond this. In combating the tendency to ontologize [*ontologisme*], when it did combat it, Western philosophy struggled for a better being, for a harmony between us and the world, or for the perfection of our own being. Its ideal of peace and equilibrium presupposed the sufficiency of being. The insufficiency of the human condition has never been understood otherwise than as a limitation of being, without our ever having envisaged the meaning of "finite being." The transcendence of these limits, communion with the infinite being, remained philosophy's sole preoccupation ... [1]

And yet modern sensibility wrestles with problems that indicate, perhaps for the first time, the abandonment of this concern with transcendence. As if it had the certainty that the idea of the limit could not apply to the *existence* of what is, but only, uniquely, to its *nature*, and as if modern sensibility perceived in being a defect still more profound. The *escape*, in regard to which contemporary literature manifests a strange disquiet, appears like a condemnation—the most radical one—of the philosophy of being by our generation.

[This term *escape*, which we borrow from the language of contemporary literary criticism, is not only a word à la mode; it is world-weariness, the disorder of our time [*mal du siècle*]. It is not easy to draw up a list of all the situations in modern life in which it shows itself. They were created in an age that leaves no one in the margins of life, and in which no one has the power to slip by himself unaware [*passer à côté de soi*]. What is caught up in the incomprehensible mechanism of the universal order is no longer the individual who does not yet belong to himself, but an autonomous person who, on the solid terrain he has conquered, feels liable to be mobilized—in every sense of the term.] Put into question, this person acquires the poignant consciousness of a final reality for which a sacrifice is asked of him. Temporal existence takes on the inexpressible flavor of the absolute. [The elementary truth that *there is being*—a being that has value and weight—is revealed at a depth that measures its brutality and its seriousness.] The pleasant game of life ceases to be just a game. It is not that the sufferings with which life threatens us render it displeasing; rather it is because the ground of suffering consists of the impossibility of interrupting it, and of an acute feeling of being held fast [*rivé*]. The impossibility of getting out of the game and of giving back to things their toy-like uselessness heralds the precise instant at which infancy comes to an end, and defines the very notion of seriousness. What counts, then, in all this experience of being, is the discovery not of a new characteristic of our existence, but of its very fact, of the permanent quality [*l'inamovibilité*][3] itself of our presence [see Rolland's Annotation 1].

Yet this revelation of being—and all it entails that is weighty and, in some sense, definitive—is at the same time the experience of a revolt. Such a revolt no longer has anything in common with what opposed the "I" to the "non-I." For the being of the "non-I" collided with our freedom, but in so doing it highlighted the exercise of that freedom. The being of the I [*moi*], which war and war's aftermath have allowed us to know, leaves us with no further games [*plus aucun jeu*]. The need to be right, or justified [*d'en avoir raison*], in this game can only be a need for escape.

Escape does not originate only from the dream of the poet who sought to evade "lower realities"; nor does it arise from the concern to break with the social conventions and constraints that falsified or annihilated our personality, as in the romantic movements of the eighteenth and nineteenth centuries. Escaping is the quest for the marvelous, which is liable to break up the somnolence of our bourgeois existence. However, it does not consist in freeing ourselves from the degrading types of servitude imposed on us by the blind mechanism of our bodies, for this is not the only possible identification between man and the nature that inspires horror in him. All these motifs are but variations on a theme whose depth they are incapable of equaling. They hold this theme within but transpose it. For these motifs do not yet place being in question, and they obey the need to transcend the limits of finite being. They translate the horror of a certain *definition* of our being but not that of being as such. The flight they command is a search for refuge. It is not only a matter of getting out [*sortir*], but also of going somewhere. On the contrary, the need for escape is found to be absolutely identical at every juncture [*point d'arrêt*] to which its adventure leads it as need; it is as though the path it traveled could not lessen its dissatisfaction.

Yet the need to escape could not be confused with the life force or the creative evolution [*devenir créateur*], which, according to a famous description, in no way fixes its ends in advance but creates them instead. Does the created being not become a burden, qua event inscribed in a destiny, for its creator? [It is precisely from all that is weighty in being that escaping sets forth] It is true that the continuous renewal of the vital urge breaks out of the prison of a present time that, scarcely actual, already becomes past, and that creation never stops with the approval of its work[but it is nonetheless the case that within the vital urge renewal is interpreted as creation and thereby denotes subservience [*asservissement*] to being. While it breaks with the rigidity of classical being, the philosophy of the vital urge does not free itself from the mystique [*prestige*] of being, for beyond the real it glimpses only the activity that creates it. It is as though the true means of surpassing the real were to consist in approximating an activity that ended up precisely with the real.

For fundamentally, becoming is not the opposite of being. The propensity toward the future and the "out-ahead-of-one-self" contained in the vital urge mark a being destined for a race-course [*voué à une course*] [see Rolland's Annotation 2]. The urge is creative but irresistible. The fulfillment of a destiny is the stigma of being: the destination is not wholly traced out, but its fulfillment is fatal, inevitable. One is at the crossroads, but one must choose. We have embarked. With the vital urge we are going toward the unknown, but we are going somewhere, whereas with escape we aspire only to get out [*sortir*]. It is this category of getting out, assimilable neither to renovation nor to creation, that we must grasp in all its purity. It is an inimitable theme that invites us to get out of being. A quest for the way out, this is in no sense a nostalgia for death because death is not a exit, just as it is not a solution. The ground of this theme is constituted—if one will pardon the neologism—by the need for *excendence*.[4] Thus, to the need for escape, being appears not only as an obstacle that free thought would have to surmount, nor even as the rigidity that, by inviting us to routine, demands an effort toward originality; rather it appears as an imprisonment from which one must get out.

Existence is an absolute that is asserted without reference to anything else. It is identity. But in this reference to himself [*soi-même*],[5] man perceives a type of duality. His identity with himself loses the character of a logical or tautological form; it takes on a dramatic form, as we will demonstrate. In the identity of the I [*moi*], the identity of being reveals its nature as enchainment, for it appears in the form of suffering and invites us to escape. Thus, escape is the need to get out of oneself, that is, *to break that most radical and unalterably binding of chains, the fact that the I [moi] is oneself [soi-même].*

Escaping therefore has little in common with that need for "innumerable lives," which is an analogous motif in modern literature, albeit totally different in its intentions. The I that wants to get out of itself [*soi-même*] does not flee itself as a limited being. It is not the fact that life is the choice and, consequently, the sacrifice of numerous possibilities that will never be realized that incites us to escape. The need for a universal or infinite existence allowing for the realization of multiple possibilities supposes a peace become real at the depths of the I, that is, the acceptance of being. Escape, on the contrary, puts in question precisely this alleged peace-with-self, since it aspires to break the chains of the I to the self [*du moi à soi*]. It is being itself or the "one-self" from which escape flees, and in no wise being's limitation. In escape the I flees itself, not in opposition to the infinity of what it is not or of what it will not become, but rather due to the very fact that it is or that it becomes. Its preoccupations go beyond the distinction of the finite and the infinite—notions, after all, that could not apply to the fact of being itself but only to its powers and properties. The ego has only the brutality of its existence in sight, which does not pose the question of infinity.

Therefore, the need for escape—whether filled with chimerical hopes or not, no matter!—leads us into the heart of philosophy. It allows us to renew the ancient problem of being qua being. What is the structure of this pure being? Does it have the universality Aristotle conferred on it? Is it the ground and the limit of our preoccupations, as certain modern philosophers would have it? On the contrary, is it nothing else than the mark of a certain civilization, firmly established in the fait accompli of being and incapable of getting out of it? And, in these conditions, is *excendence* possible, and how would it be accomplished? What is the ideal of happiness and human dignity that it promises [see Rolland's Annotation 3]?

II

Yet is the need for escape not the exclusive matter of a finite being? Does this being not aspire to cross the limits of being rather than to flee being as being? Would an infinite being have the need to take leave of itself? Is this infinite being not precisely the ideal of self-sufficiency and the promise of eternal contentment?

That would suppose that need is just a privation. Perhaps we shall manage to show that there is in need something other than a lack. Moreover, the notions of the finite and the infinite apply only to *that which is*; they lack precision when applied to *the being* of that which is. *That which is* necessarily possesses a greater or lesser range of possibilities, over which it is master. Properties can have relations with other properties and be measured against an ideal of perfection. The very fact of existing refers only to itself. It is that through which all powers and all properties are posited. The escape we envisage should look to us like the inner structure of this fact of self-positing [*le fait de se poser*]. We will attempt to discover escape in a state of affairs where the fact of self-positing is laid bare, freed from any consideration of natures, qualities, or powers that are posited and that mask the event through which they *are*. But how shall we take account of the finite or the infinite in the fact of positing? Is there a more or less perfect manner of being posited? What is, is. The fact of being is always already perfect. It is already inscribed in the absolute. That there might have been a birth or a death in no way affects the absolute character of an assertion that refers only to itself. This is why we believe that the problem of the origin and death could not be judiciously posed until the analysis of escape was completed. In this introduction, we shall not lose interest in that thematic. Moreover, escape will not appear to us as a flight toward death or as a stepping outside of time. We will reserve for another study the demonstration of the ontologistic character[6] of nothingness and eternity.

In the meantime, it is worth our while to describe the structure of need. After what we have just said about the notion of being, it is clear that even if the ground of need were to consist in a lack, then this lack could not affect the "existence of the existent," to which one can neither add nor remove anything. In reality, need is intimately tied to being, but not in the quality of privation. On the contrary, need will allow us to discover, not a limitation of that being that desires to surpass its limits in order to enrich and fulfill itself, but rather the purity of the fact of being, which already looks like an escape.

The essential work of this study is devoted to that analysis.

III

In the first place, need seems to aspire only to its own satisfaction. The search for satisfaction becomes the search for the object able to procure it. Need thus turns us toward something other than ourselves. Therefore, it appears upon initial analysis like an insufficiency in our being, impelled to seek refuge in something other than itself. An insufficiency habitually interpreted as a lack, it would indicate some weakness of our human constitution, or the limitation of our being. The malaise by which need begins and which somehow innervates or animates it—even when it attains only a moderate intensity—would be the affective translation of this finitude. Likewise, the pleasure of satisfaction would express the reestablishment of a natural plenitude.

And yet this whole psychology of need is a bit hasty. It too quickly interprets the insufficiency of need as an insufficiency of being. Thus it assumes a metaphysics in which need is characterized in advance as an emptiness in a world where the real is identified with the full. That is an identification that threatens any thinking that could not distinguish between existence and the existent, all thinking that applies to the one what should instead have meaning for the other.

Need becomes imperious only when it becomes suffering. And the specific mode of suffering that characterizes need is malaise, or disquiet.

Malaise is not a purely passive state, resting upon itself. The fact of being ill at ease [*mal à son aise*] is essentially dynamic. It appears as a refusal to remain in place, as an effort to get out of an unbearable situation. What constitutes its particular character, however, is the indeterminacy of the goal that this departure sets for itself, which should be seen as a positive characteristic. It is an attempt to get out without knowing where one is going, and this ignorance qualifies the very essence of this attempt.

There are needs for which the consciousness of a well-determined object—susceptible of satisfying those needs—is lacking. The needs that we do not lightly call "intimate" remain at the stage of a malaise, which is surmounted in a state closer to deliverance than to satisfaction.

To be sure, it is not usually this way. But only extrinsic experiences and lessons can give to need the knowledge of the object liable to satisfy it, just as they add ideas about the need's value. Therefore, the increasing specialization of needs and the consciousness of their objects, which itself grows clearer and clearer, more and more refined, develop only as a function of learning and education. However unreflective this consciousness may be, it is the consciousness of objects; it places our being under the tutelage of what is outside of us. The whole problem consists in knowing whether the fundamental preoccupation with need is thereby explained, whether the satisfaction of need responds precisely to the disquiet of malaise.

Now, the suffering of need in no way indicates a lack to be filled; this suffering does not expose us as finite beings. The being that has not satisfied its needs dies. But this indisputable statement has an extrinsic origin. In itself, need does not foreshadow the end. It clings fiercely to the present, which then appears at the threshold of a possible future. One heartrending need is the despair over a death that does not come.

Moreover, the satisfaction of a need does not destroy it. Not only are needs reborn, but disappointment also follows their satisfaction. We are in no way neglecting the fact that satisfaction appeases need. However, it is a matter of knowing whether this ideal of peace lies within the initial demands of need itself. We note in the phenomenon of malaise a different and perhaps superior demand: a kind of dead weight in the depths of our being, whose satisfaction does not manage to rid us of it.

What gives the human condition all its importance is precisely this inadequacy of satisfaction to need. The justification of certain ascetic tendencies lies there: the mortifications of fasting are not only agreeable to God; they bring us closer to the situation that is the fundamental event of our being: the need for escape.

We are thus moving toward the thesis of the inadequacy of satisfaction to need. The analysis of the satisfaction of need and of the atmosphere in which it is brought about will lead us to attribute to need a type of insufficiency to which satisfaction could never respond.

IV

To justify our thesis that need expresses the presence of our being and not its deficiency, we must look at the primordial phenomenon of need's satisfaction: pleasure.

It is certainly not to the materiality of the objects liable to satisfy need that he who feels it is oriented. Their possible use alone interests him. But there is more to this. Satisfaction is fulfilled in an atmosphere of fever and exaltation, which allows us to say that need is a search for pleasure. What does this pleasure signify?

The moralists' contempt for pleasure is matched only by the attraction it exerts upon human beings. And yet within pleasure's specific dynamism—likewise unknown to the moralists, who present it as a state—the satisfaction of need comes

to pass. But another game unfolds around the process that results in need's appeasement, one that philosophers deprecate as
mere accompaniment but that human beings take seriously.

Pleasure appears as it develops. It is neither there as a
whole, nor does it happen all at once. And furthermore, it will
never be whole or integral. Progressive movement is a characteristic trait of this phenomenon, which is by no means a simple state. This is a movement that does not tend toward a goal,
for it has no end. It exists wholly in the enlargement of its own
amplitude, which is like the rarefaction of our existence [*être*],
or its swooning. In the very depths of incipient pleasure there
opens something like abysses, ever deeper, into which our existence, no longer resisting, hurls itself. There is something dizzying to pleasure's unfolding [*devenir*]. There is ease or cowardice.
The [human] being feels its substance somehow draining from
it; it grows lighter, as if drunk, and disperses.

Pleasure is, in effect, nothing less than a concentration in
the instant. Aristippus's hedonism is chimerical because he allows for an indivisible present, possessed in pleasure. But it is
precisely the instant that is split up in pleasure. It loses its solidity and its consistency, and each of its parts is enriched with
new potentialities for swooning as the ecstasy intensifies. The
magnitude of the force alone measures the intensity of pleasure; pain is concentration. The instant is not recaptured until
the moment when pleasure is broken, after the supreme break,
when the [human] being believed in complete ecstasy but was
completely disappointed, and is entirely disappointed and
ashamed to find himself again existing.

We therefore note in pleasure an abandonment, a loss of
oneself, a getting out of oneself, an ecstasy: so many traits that
describe the promise of escape contained in pleasure's essence.
Far from appearing like a passive state, pleasure opens a di-

mension in the satisfaction of need in which malaise glimpses an escape. Therefore, need is not a nostalgia for being; it is the liberation from being, since the movement of pleasure is precisely the loosening of the malaise.

Moreover, the very fact that the satisfaction of need is accompanied by an affective event reveals the true meaning of need. There is no simple *act* that could fill the lack announced in need. In effect, the simple act presupposes a constituted being; it is not the affirmation itself of that being. Affectivity, on the contrary, is foreign to notions that apply to that which is, and has never been reducible to categories of thought and activity.

Aristotle had an acute sense of pleasure's foreignness to activity. Yet it is not true that pleasure is added to the act, "like the flower to youth," for this rather unsuggestive image reduces pleasure to the level of a state; it conceals the movement of pleasure in which satisfaction comes to pass and with it the promise of escape that it brings to the malaise of need. It is nevertheless fair to say that pleasure is not the goal of need, for pleasure is not an end [*terme*]. Pleasure is a process; it is the process of departing from being [*processus de sortie de l'être*]. Its affective nature is not only the expression or the sign of this getting-out; it is the getting out itself. Pleasure is affectivity, precisely because it does not take on the forms of being, but rather attempts to break these up. Yet it is a deceptive escape.

For it is an escape that fails. If, like a process that is far from closing up on itself, pleasure appears in a constant surpassing of oneself, it breaks just at the moment where it seems to get out absolutely. It develops with an increase in promises, which become richer the closer it comes to its paroxysm, but these promises are never kept.

Thus antiquity's notion of mixed pleasures contains a great part of truth. It is not the fact of being conditioned by need and mixed with pain that compromises its purity. In itself, on a strictly affective level, pleasure is disappointment and deceit. It is not disappointment through the role it plays in life, or through its destructive effects, or even through its moral indignity, but rather through its internal unfolding [*devenir interne*].

Pleasure conforms to the demands of need but is incapable of equaling them. And, at the moment of its disappointment, which should have been that of its triumph, the meaning of its failure is underscored by shame [see Rolland's Annotation 4].

V

On first analysis, shame appears to be reserved for phenomena of a moral order: one feels ashamed for having acted badly, for having deviated from the norm. It is the representation we form of ourselves as diminished beings with which we are pained to identify. Yet shame's whole intensity, everything it contains that stings us, consists precisely in our inability not to identify with this being who is already foreign to us and whose motives for acting we can no longer comprehend.

This first description, albeit superficial, reveals to us that shame is more attached to the being of our I than it is to its finitude. Shame does not depend—as we might believe—on the limitation of our being, inasmuch as it is liable to sin [*susceptible de péché*], but rather on the very being of our being, on its incapacity to break with itself. Shame is founded upon the solidarity of our being, which obliges us to claim responsibility for ourselves.

Nevertheless, this analysis of shame is insufficient, for it presents shame as a function of a determinate act, a morally bad act. It is important that we free shame from this condition.

Shame arises each time we are unable to make others forget [*faire oublier*] our basic nudity. It is related to everything we would like to hide and that we cannot bury or cover up. The timid man who is all arms and legs is ultimately incapable of covering the nakedness of his physical presence with his moral person. Poverty is not a vice, but it is shameful because, like the beggar's rags, it shows up the nakedness of an existence incapable of hiding itself. This preoccupation with dressing to hide ourselves concerns every manifestation of our lives, our acts, and our thoughts. We accede to the world through words, and we want them to be noble. It is the great merit of Céline's *Journey to the End of the Night*, thanks to a marvelous flair for language, to have undressed the universe in a sad and desperate cynicism.

In shameful nakedness, what is thus in question is not only the body's nakedness. However, it is not by pure chance that, under the poignant form of modesty, shame is primarily connected to our body. For what is the meaning of shameful nakedness? It is this that one seeks to hide from the others, but also from oneself. This aspect of shame is often ignored. We see in shame its social aspect; we forget that its deepest manifestations are an eminently personal matter. If shame is present, it means that we cannot hide what we should like to hide. The necessity of fleeing, in order to hide oneself, is put in check by the impossibility of fleeing oneself. What appears in shame is thus precisely the fact of being riveted to oneself, the radical impossibility of fleeing oneself to hide from oneself, the unalterably binding presence of the I to itself [*du moi à soi-même*] [see Rolland's Annotation 5]. Nakedness is shameful when it is the sheer visibility [*patence*] of our being, of its ultimate intimacy. And the nakedness of our body is not that of a material thing, antithesis of spirit, but the nakedness of our total being in all its fullness and solidity, of its most brutal expression of which we could not fail to take note. The whistle that Charlie Chaplin swallows in *City Lights* triggers the scandal of the brutal presence of his being; it works like a recording device, which betrays the discrete manifestations of a presence that Charlie's legendary tramp costume barely dissimulates. When the body loses this character of intimacy, this character of the existence of a self, it ceases to become shameful. Consider the naked body of the boxer. The nakedness of the music hall dancer, who exhibits herself—to whatever effect desired by the impresario—is not necessarily the mark of a shameless being, for her body appears to her with that exteriority to self that serves as a form of cover. Being naked is not a question of wearing clothes.

It is therefore our intimacy, that is, our presence to ourselves, that is shameful. It reveals not our nothingness but rather the totality of our existence. Nakedness is the need to excuse one's existence. Shame is, in the last analysis, an existence that seeks excuses. What shame discovers [*découvre*] is the being who *uncovers* himself [*se* découvre].

Thus modesty penetrates need, which has already appeared to us as the very malaise of being and, at bottom, as the fundamental category of existence. And modesty does not leave need once the latter is satisfied.[7] The being who has gorged himself falls back into the agonizing disappointment of his shameful intimacy, for he finds himself anew after the vanity of his pleasure.

However, to defend the thesis according to which being is, at bottom, a weight for itself, we must focus still more closely on the phenomenon of malaise.

VI

Let us analyze a case in which the nature of malaise appears in all its purity and to which the word "malaise" applies par excellence: nausea.[8] The state of nausea that precedes vomiting, and from which vomiting will deliver us, encloses us on all sides. Yet it does not come from outside to confine us. We are revolted from the inside; our depths smother beneath ourselves; our innards "heave" [*nous avons "mal au cœur"*].

When considered in the instant in which it is lived and in the atmosphere that surrounds it, this revolting presence of ourselves to ourselves appears insurmountable. Yet in the conflict and duality thus suggested between us and the nauseated state, we could not qualify the latter as an obstacle. That image would falsify and impoverish the true state of things. The obstacle is outside the effort that surpasses it. When the obstacle is insurmountable, this characteristic is added to its nature qua obstacle, but it does not modify this nature, just as our sentiment of its immensity removes nothing from the object's externality. We can still turn away from it. Nausea, on the contrary, sticks to us. Yet it would not be correct to say that nausea is an obstacle that we cannot dodge. That would again be to maintain a duality between us and it, leaving aside a sui generis implication that characterizes this duality and to which we will return.

There is in nausea a refusal to remain there, an effort to get out. Yet this effort is always already characterized as desperate: in any case, it is so for any attempt to act or to think. And this despair, this fact of being riveted, constitutes all the anxiety of nausea. In nausea—which amounts to an impossibility of being what one is—we are at the same time riveted to ourselves, enclosed in a tight circle that smothers. We are there, and there is nothing more to be done, or anything to add to this fact that we have been entirely delivered up, that everything is consumed: *this is the very experience of pure being*, which we have promised from the beginning of this work. However, this "nothing-more-to-be-done" is the mark of a limit-situation in which the uselessness of any action is precisely the sign of the supreme instant from which we can only depart. The experience of pure being is at the same time the experience of its internal antagonism and of the escape that foists itself on us.

Nevertheless, death is not the exit toward which escape thrusts us. Death can only appear to it if escape reflects upon itself. As such, nausea discovers only the nakedness of being in its plenitude and in its utterly binding presence.

This is why nausea is shameful in a particularly significant form. It is not only shameful because it threatens to offend social conventions. The social aspect of shame is fainter in nausea, and all the shameful manifestations of our body, than it is in any morally wrong act. The shameful manifestations of our bodies compromise us in a manner totally different than does the lie or dishonesty. The fault consists not in the lack of propriety but almost in the very fact of having a body, of being there [see Rolland's Annotation 6]. In nausea, shame appears purified of any admixture of collective representations. When nausea is experienced in solitude, its compromising character, far from effacing itself, appears in all its originality. The sick person in isolation, who "was taken ill" [*s'est trouvé mal*] and who has no choice but to vomit, is still "scandalized" by himself. The presence of another is even desired, to a certain degree, for it allows the scandal of nausea to be brought down to the level of an "illness," of a fact that is socially normal and can be treated, and in regard to which one can consequently adopt an objective attitude [see Rolland's Annotation 7]. The phenomenon of shame of a self confronted with itself, discussed above, is the same as nausea.

But is nausea not a fact of consciousness, which the I knows as one of its states? Is this *existence* itself, or only an *existent*? In so asking, we forget the sui generis implication that constitutes nausea, which allows us to see in it the fulfillment of the very being of the entity that we are [*l'accomplissement de l'être même de l'étant que nous sommes*]. For what constitutes the relationship between nausea and us is nausea itself. The binding, or irremissible, quality of nausea constitutes its very ground. Despair over this ineluctable presence constitutes the presence itself. Thereby, nausea posits itself not only as something absolute, but as the very act of self-positing: it is the affirmation itself of being. It refers only to itself, is closed to all the rest, without windows onto other things. Nausea carries its center of attraction within itself. And the ground of this position consists in impotence before its own reality, which nevertheless constitutes that reality itself. Therefore, one might say, nausea reveals to us the presence of being in all its impotence, which constitutes this presence as such. It is the impotence of pure being, in all its nakedness. Therefore, ultimately, nausea also appears as a fact of consciousness that is "exceptional." If, in every psychological fact, the existence of the fact of consciousness gets confused with its knowledge, if the conscious fact is known by way of its existence, nevertheless its nature does not merge with its presence. On the other hand, the nature of nausea is nothing other than its presence, nothing other than our powerlessness to take leave of that presence.

Powerlessness to take leave of that presence

nausea is it's presence

VII

It thus appears that at the root of need there is not a lack of being but, on the contrary, a plenitude of being. Need is not oriented toward the complete fulfillment of a limited being, toward satisfaction, but toward release and escape. Hence, to assume an infinite being [*un être infini*] that would have no need is a *contradictio in adjecto*. The experience that reveals to us the presence of being as such, the pure existence of being, is an experience of its powerlessness, the source of all need. That powerlessness therefore appears neither as a limit to being nor as the expression of a finite being. The "imperfection" of being does not appear as identical to its limitation. Being is "imperfect" inasmuch as it is being, and not inasmuch as it is finite. If, by the finitude of a being, we understand the fact that it is a burden to itself and that it aspires to escape, then the notion of finite being is a tautology. Being is thus essentially finite [see Rolland's Annotation 8].

The banal observation that man is by birth engaged in an existence he neither willed nor chose must not be limited to the case of man as a finite being. He translates the structure of being itself. The fact of beginning to exist is not a matter of inevitability, for inevitability obviously already presupposes existence. The entry into existence did not vex some will, since in that case the existence of that will would have come before itself [*aurait préexisté à son existence*]. And yet the feeling of the brutality of existence is not some mere illusion of a finite being that, taking stock of itself, would measure the fact of its existence by the faculties and powers it possesses qua already existing. If these powers and faculties appear to it as essentially limited, then their limitation belongs to an order other than that of the brutality of existence. That limitation could only be fundamentally foreign to the plane where a will can collide with obstacles or be subject to tyranny. For limitation is the mark of the existence of the existent.[9] This weight of the being that is crushed by itself, which we revealed in the phenomenon of malaise, this condemnation to be oneself, can also be seen in the dialectical impossibility of conceiving the beginning of being—that is, of grasping the moment where being takes up this weight—and of being nevertheless driven back to the problem of one's origin. It is not that this origin is incomprehensible because it emerged from nothingness, contrary to the rules of fabrication, for it is absurd to postulate, among the conditions of being, those of a work that presupposes it as already constituted. To set behind being a creator who is also conceived as a being also fails to posit the beginning of being outside the conditions of an already constituted being.[10] It is in the being that begins—not in its relations with its cause—that we find the paradox of a being that begins to be, or, in other words, the impossibility of distinguishing, in this being, what takes on the weight [of being] from that weight itself. This difficulty does not disappear with the demise of the prejudice according to which being was preceded by nothingness.

Henri Bergson has shown that to think nothingness is to think of being as crossed out.[11] And it seems to us incontestable that nothingness is the work of a thinking essentially turned toward being. But thereby we get no solution to the problem that lies elsewhere: Is being sufficient unto itself? The problem of the origin of being is not the problem of its proceeding out of nothingness, but that of its sufficiency or insufficiency. This problem is dictated by all that is revolting in the positing of being.

Moreover, the paradox of being remains intact when we free ourselves of time and grant ourselves eternity. We will reserve the problem of eternity for a later study, which will have to sketch the philosophy of escape. But let us say straightaway that it is not in view of eternity that escape is made. Eternity is just the intensification, or radicalization, of the fatality of that being, which is riveted to itself [*lui-même*]. And there is a deep truth in the myth that says that eternity weighs heavily upon the immortal gods [see Rolland's Annotation 9].

VIII

And yet progress has not brought Western philosophy to surpass being entirely. When it discovered, beyond things, the realms of the ideal, of consciousness, and of becoming—our first model of being—it was incapable of denying these realms an existence, since the benefit of its discovery consisted precisely in making them be. Ontologism in its broadest meaning remained the fundamental dogma of all thought. Despite all its subtlety, it remained prisoner of an elementary and simple principle, according to which one could think and feel only that which exists or is supposed to exist. A principle more imperious than that of non-contradiction, since here nothingness itself—to the degree that thinking encounters it—gets clothed with existence, and so we must without restriction state, against Parmenides, that non-being is.

Perhaps making a distinction between the form and the matter of thinking will allow us to escape an accusation that utterly burdens thinking with an absurdity. Is the positing [*position*] contained in all theoretical thought not distinct from the assertion of being? Does the pure form of an object—which everything that thinking thinks must take on—already transform this matter into a being? However that may be, the form of the object is conceived on the model of being, and the affirmation of possible existence is contained in the copula. The object is a possibility of existence, and whatever the difficulty in attributing a possible existence to nothingness, the attachment of thought to being is unshakable [*indefectible*].

Moreover, contemplative thought, or theory, is at bottom the behavior of him who forever carries the mark [*stigmate*] of existence: theory is essentially subservient to the existent and, when it does not start from being, it anticipates it. This is the powerlessness before the fait accompli. Knowledge [*connaissance*] is precisely that which remains to be done when everything is completed.

The behavior of the creature, confined in the fait accompli of creation, did not remain outside of attempts at escaping. The urge toward the Creator expressed a taking leave of being. But philosophy either applied the category of being to God or contemplated him as the Creator, as though one could surpass being by approaching an activity or by imitating a work that led precisely to being. The romanticism of creative activity is animated by the profound need to get out of being, yet all the same it shows an attachment to its created essence and its eyes are fixed on being. For this romanticism, the problem of God has remained that of his existence [see Rolland's Annotation 10].

In this universality of being for thought and for action resides traditional idealism's impotence before the persistent return of a doctrine that rightly recalls the fundamental attachment to being of the thinking whose task was to surpass it. In its opposition to realism, the idealism of thought modifies the structure of the existent but does not tackle its existence. Thought cannot say anything about this and leaves the task of interpreting existence to all those who ask only not to go beyond being [*qui ne demandent qu'à ne pas aller*]. The emancipation of idealism in regard to being is based upon its undervaluation. Consequently, at the very moment when idealism

idealism always finds being

imagines it has surpassed being, it is invaded by being from all
sides. Those intellectual relations into which idealism dissolved
the universe are no less its existences—neither inert nor
opaque, to be sure—and they do not escape the laws of being.
Idealism is exposed not only to the attacks of all who charge it
with sacrificing sensuous reality and with ignoring or scorning
the concrete and poignant demands of human beings prey to
their everyday problems. Consequently, idealism is charged
with being unable to command and to guide. But it does not
even have the excuse of escaping from being. Indeed, at the
level to which it leads us, idealism finds being—in a subtler
form, one that beckons us to a false serenity—always the same,
having relinquished none of its characteristics.

And yet the value of European civilization consists incontestably in the aspirations of idealism, if not in its path: in its
primary inspiration idealism seeks to surpass being. Every civilization that accepts being—with the tragic despair it contains
and the crimes it justifies—merits the name "barbarian" [see
Rolland's Annotation 11].

Consequently, the only path open for us to satisfy idealism's legitimate demands without nevertheless entering into its
erring ways is that on which we measure without fear all the
weight of being and its universality. It is the path where we recognize the inanity of acts and thoughts incapable of taking the
place of an event that breaks up existence in the very accomplishment of its existence. Such deeds and thoughts must not
conceal from us, then, the originality of escape. It is a matter of
getting out of being by a new path, at the risk of overturning
certain notions that to common sense and the wisdom of the
nations seemed the most evident [see Rolland's Annotation 12].

Annotations
Jacques Rolland

1. This dimension of existence, perceived in the sentiment of being riveted, in that of being's nonremittable obligation or of its nonremovable quality, has been traced back, in the introduction, to its probable philosophical origin, the Heideggerian notion of *Geworfenheit.* But the reflection on the body leads us to wonder, nevertheless, whether it might not have yet another origin: Jewishness—in the sense in which Nazi anti-Semitism was able brutally to unveil, during these years, its precisely nonremittable quality. We must return to this. We are thinking of an article Levinas published in 1935, in issue number 8 of the journal of the Alliance Israélite Universelle, *Paix et Droit*: "The Religious Inspiration of the Alliance."[1] We might note the following few sentences: "Hitlerism is the greatest trial—an incomparable trial—through which Judaism has had to pass. . . . The pathetic destiny of being Jewish becomes a fatality. One can no longer flee it. The Jew is ineluctably riveted to his Judaism" (p. 4). A youth "definitively attached to the sufferings

and joys of the nations to which it belongs . . . discovers in the
reality of Hitlerism all the gravity of being Jewish"; "In the bar-
barous and primitive symbol of race . . . Hitler recalled that
one does not desert Judaism."

The language of these sentences cannot fail to strike us by
its similarity with that used by "On Escape" to state the manner by which the existent is compelled to its existence. Coming from a man who will later emphasize the prephilosophical
experiences that are the sap from which philosophical reflection is nourished, this expression of a "prephilosophical experience," fundamental at the least, of the trauma provoked by the
first manifestations of racial anti-Semitism, cannot fail to keep
us alert.

We have noted in the introduction that "On Escape" could
be understood as an essay "in the hermeneutics of facticity,"
tarrying at the level of *Geworfenheit* and, by virtue of this pause
[*cet arrêt*], diverging from the course pursued by the Heideggerian meditation. Why this pause? A single response is possible: because it allows us to grasp (or at least to advance toward)
the meaning of existence in its totality, just as, in Heidegger, it
is the opposition between *Geworfenheit* and *Entwurf* [thrown-
ness and projecting] that sets us en route toward this understanding. Yet in order that *Geworfenheit*, or the fact of being
riveted to an existence one has not chosen, appear as the un-
surpassable ground and, thence, the ultimate meaning of existence such as this ontology alone can understand it, *it is necessary that existence assert itself as Geworfenheit*, in the fatality of
being-riveted to that which one cannot desert. Might one not
think, then, that it is the brutal revelation of being-Jewish, as
being-riveted-to-Judaism as to that which one cannot desert,
that has led to thinking being-human as such as being-riveted-
to-being in all the gravity of the fact of being, and to elaborat-

ing that thought philosophically while tarrying, in description, at the "moment" of *Geworfenheit*? (But being-riveted-to-Judaism is not identified with that for which it would be the model here, i.e., being-riveted-to-being; for it is election in a positive sense, that is, as service, but thereby already an ethical deliverance relative to being understood as a "race course" [*course*]. This was indicated already in a text just subsequent to the period we are concerned with here, "The Spiritual Essence of Anti-Semitism According to Jacques Maritain," published in *Paix et Droit* [issue 5], in 1938 [pp. 3–4]. Thus, "Foreign to the world, the Jew would be its ferment; he would awaken it from its torpor, he would communicate to it his own impatience and concern over the good." The compulsion, like tension, does not have here being as its object, but rather the Good, that is, as the later work will teach us, that which, beyond being, is *better* than being.)

This does not amount, in our mind, to losing ourselves in anecdotes. These reflections refer instead to a thinking that is present at the depths of the collection of "Essays on Judaism," entitled *Difficult Freedom*.[2] This is a thinking according to which being-Jewish—the fact that something like this could exist in the world and not only in the gaze of the anti-Semite, as Sartre would have it, but rather according to its own modalities—is not itself an empirical fact but rather constitutes a structure of mind and meaning, "an extreme possibility, of impossibility" of human existence as such. This is a possibility that means the "break with the naïveté of the herald, the messenger, or the shepherd of being of an *ethical* humanity." In his last years, Levinas spoke of this in terms of the possibility of the seated man. He did not mean thereby what Nietzsche detested in Flaubert, but rather the story of Jacob, who, unlike Esau, "the man who knew hunting," became a "complete man" who "lived in tents," where he sat to study the Book and to invent, before its time, the famous *Lernen* (cf. Genesis 25:27). But, on the basis of this "structural" interpretation of being-Jewish, anti-Semitism itself and the judeocide to which it led in this past century also cease to be merely empirical facts.[3]

2. Though this passage in its entirety clearly refers to Bergson, in this sentence the presence of Heidegger, for whom *Dasein* is defined precisely by its being-out-ahead-of-oneself, is just as undeniable. What thus becomes altogether interesting is the equivalence established through the sentence's phrasing, between being-out-ahead-of-oneself and being-devoted-to-a-racecourse. This equivalence refers us to recent texts where Levinas takes with radical seriousness the obligation to be [*l'astriction à être*] that characterizes the *Dasein* and that amounts to a "reduction of the human to the task of being." "The ess*a*nce of being or *being-in-question* is in question in the being-there as *having-to-be*, which is the being of man. *Man is*: this is equivalent to man *has* to be. The 'property' indicated in the *having* [*avoir*] of the having-to-be [*de l'avoir-à-être*] measures all that which is irrecusable—irrecusable *to the point of dying*—in the strict obligation to be, included in the *to* of the *to be*."[4] But from there we can also see the (surprising) proximity of the *Dasein* understood this way to Spinoza's *conatus essendi*. The latter term reappears frequently in Levinas's recent texts. It designates the strain on the self, the race toward this self out-ahead of oneself, the "epic of being" of a being persevering in its being, when the latter is no longer defined as "actual essence" but rather dynamically, as *having-to-be* or as the task of being.

3. We did not pause in the introduction over the contents of this series of questions, but were satisfied simply to signal their importance. We must do so here, briefly.

—Universality will be effectively accredited to being (farther on, on page 99, we will be told that it is appropriate to "measure without fear all the weight of being and its universality")—but in a sense radically marked anew by the Heideggerian return of its ontological or verbal sense.

—Heidegger, who reappears in the following question, since we cannot fail to see in him the first of these "modern philosophers" from whom Levinas wants to distance himself insofar as they see in being "the ground and limit of our preoccupations." Is he not, nevertheless, accompanied by Husserl, such as Levinas's *Theory of Intuition* reads him; that is, in light of the teaching of *Being and Time*?[5]

—The idea of "ontological imperialism" as "the mark of a certain civilization" will reappear toward the end of the essay (98); it is at that point that we will speak of it.

—The possibility and modality of getting out, of escape, of the "excendence," constitute in effect the central question of this essay. A central question that nonetheless, as we attempted to show in the introduction, persists in the background, and regardless will remain there without response. Let us simply recall here that the later work, in its entirety, can be read as the effort—both continuous in inspiration and multiple (i.e., discontinuous) in its manner—to answer this question, and even to elaborate it as a question.

—Happiness and dignity: two words that occupy a quite marginal place in the Levinasian lexicon. The first word alone is the object of analysis in *Totality and Infinity*, where it rests upon the immediacy of enjoyment. It is evidently not this sense that is intended here. In ethics, happiness can only signify the happiness of the other *for whom* I am, a happiness of the other that is demanded of me in such a way, moreover, that in striving to realize it, I am not practicing a virtue that would already promise to be allied to my own happiness. We could not be less

Kantian here! However, what does stand out against the horizon of ethical practice—at the farthest distance from any claim and any hope for a happiness liable to become my own—would be, precisely, dignity: the dignity of a responsible subject, that is, a subject uninterested in remuneration. This is the dignity without appeal of an attachment to the "Good that is not pleasant, which commands and prescribes." And Levinas will write much later, "The obedience to prescription . . . implies no other reward than this very elevation of the dignity of soul; and disobedience implies no punishment if not that of the rupture itself with the Good. A service indifferent to remuneration!"[6]

Yet how can we not think of Blanchot here when he writes, "It is as if he said, 'May happiness come for all, on condition that, through this wish, I be excluded from it.'"[7]

4. This phenomenology of pleasure seems to call for three remarks:

—It is perhaps not without interest to note that this "reading" of pleasure as progressive movement on the one hand, and as tied, on the other, to "getting out," will be presented anew [forty years later], as though he had just turned a page, in *Otherwise than Being or Beyond Essence*. We are thinking of the quite remarkable note on page 8, whose last two sentences we transcribe here: "It is the superlative, more than the negation of categories, that interrupts systems, as though the logical order and the being it succeeds in espousing retained the superlative which exceeds them: in subjectivity the superlative is the exorbitance of a null-site, in caresses and in sexuality there is the 'over-bid' of tangency—as though tangency admitted degrees—up to contact with the entrails, a skin going under another skin."[8]

—A reading that should probably permit us to understand in all its significance the "erotic literature" of, say, Bataille. For, in Bataille, eroticism in its most pornographic forms and its crudest expression only has "meaning" in "piercing the heart of the sky."[9] Eroticism as disaster—and as dis-aster![10] Rupture of the possible, of the known, in Bataille's vocabulary; a rift inscribed in being, a slackening of the noose that is being-one-self [*l'être-soi-même*], such as he would have us think it. Pleasure has ultimately but one language; it is that of the "Mother": "Let me sway with you in this joy, which is the certainty of an abyss more complete, more violent, than any desire."[11] Yet the same mouth states that this pleasure, in its most exaggerated forms—all the way to the monstrous—may go by itself to its own failure. "I know," she said, "that you will survive me and that, in surviving me, you will betray an abominable mother. . . . The ecstasy [*volupté*] in which you are sinking is already so great that I can tell you: it will be followed by your undoing."[12]

It is clear that here only death could fulfill the promise of escape that pleasure carries with it and that, conversely, mere survival is its betrayal. But precisely in Bataille—and this is, no doubt, what makes the atmosphere of this literature so hard to read—what follows pleasure is not death but sleep, a sleep as heavy as that of the Baudelairean assassin, out of which one steps, dazed and sick, toward the *awaiting* [*pour l'attente*], the "long awaiting of death."[13]

—Yet the failure inscribed in the very unfolding [*le devenir même*] of pleasure again makes inevitable one of its essential traits (massively present in Bataille moreover): *repetition*. Whence pleasure's affinity with desire, such as Hegel describes it at the beginning of the chapter "The Actualization of Self-Consciousness" in the *Phenomenology of Spirit*.[14] But whence also its affinity with writing as repetitions, returns, recommencements dulling the sharp edge of every beginning, that is, such as Blanchot thinks it. We must break with all that in order to think about an escape that does not fail, as it were—that is, with desire, such as it is in play in literature and erotics. But this signifies arriving at what *Totality and Infinity* designated as *metaphysical desire*: a desire without deception, without the return to its point of departure, a desire not harassed by repetition—because it is a desire that is not oriented toward satisfaction.

Desire is desire for the absolutely Other. Outside of the hunger that we satisfy, of the thirst we quench, and the senses we calm, metaphysics desires the Other beyond satisfactions, without there being any gesture possible, by the body, to diminish its aspiration; without it being possible to sketch any known caress or invent any new caress. This is desire without satisfaction that, precisely, understands the distance, the alterity, and the exteriority of the Other. For Desire, this alterity has a meaning, one inadequate to its idea. It is understood as the alterity of the Other person and as that of the Most-High. The very dimension of height is opened by metaphysical Desire. That this height is no longer that of the sky but of the Invisible represents the very elevation of height and its nobility. To die for the invisible, that is metaphysics. But that does not mean that desire can abstain from acts. It only means that these acts are neither consummations, nor caress, nor liturgy.[15]

But this again means expressing it in this way, passing from an "erotic stage" to an "ethical stage," which for Levinas, moreover, contains the religious within itself, *because the religious does not signify outside of ethics.*

5. One will have noticed the multiplication of reflexive verbs in these lines. This multiplication cannot fail to evoke for

us the reflexive structure of emotion in *Being and Time*, which Levinas emphasized in a recent text.

The fear for another, as a fear for the death of the neighbor, is my fear, but it is in no wise fear *for* me. It thus contrasts with the admirable phenomenological analysis of affectivity that *Being and Time* proposes: a reflected structure where emotion is always an emotion *about* something moving, but also emotion *for* oneself, in which emotion consists in being moved, in being frightened, in being delighted, in becoming sad, etc. Here we find a double "intentionality" of the *about* and the *for*, participating in the emotion *par excellence*—in anguish; being-for-death, where the finite being is moved *by* its finitude *for* this same finitude.[16]

Nevertheless, here, between the Heideggerian anxiety and the Levinasian fear, a third movement is sketched, itself characterized by reflexivity turning into *passivity*. The reflexivity inherent in the attempt to hide *oneself* from *oneself* [*se* cacher à *soi-même*], and to flee *oneself*, is transformed, in the inevitable failure of this movement, into the discovery of *being riveted*, in all its passivity. This is a passivity that we must already indeed call "more passive than any passivity," since what marks and distinguishes it is the absence, within it, of an instance or moment through which what is suffered [*pâti*] would be received again and assumed. A passivity that will be grasped through the description of insomnia (see *Existence and Existents*, p. 109–113), before receiving its ethical sense by way of its inscription in the plot of signification (see *Otherwise than Being*, pp. 207–10 and our introduction, pp. 163–65).

6. Would we have rediscovered here Anaximander's ancient intuition, at least such as the young Nietzsche read it, in light of Schopenhauer's pessimism?[17] In fact, such a comparison

could only distance us from what is most interesting in the remark, which concerns, for human beings, their way of relating
to being and to their own being. What is shown here is a questioning, as it were, not of being in the being-there or *Da-sein*
(see Annotation 2 above), but rather that of the being-there in
its being. This is a putting into question that interrupts, in
some fashion, the race wherein it fulfills its task of being,
through having-to-be [*ayant-à-être*]. An interruption by which
the movement of this race no longer follows its straight path
but in some sense turns back toward him who "ran"—and in
this way deports or deflects him from his trajectory and, finally,
from any site. That then is shame: the discovery—in this halting, in this deportation—of our own presence as unjustified
and already possibly at fault. This is like a fracture in time, or
in its projection toward the future, like the opening of a sort of
present that seems no longer able to finish unless shame itself
is lifted. But from this, for shame itself, grasped "in the moment in which it is experienced," we have a present that we
must call without-end, like Blanchot's suffering, evoked in our
introduction. And from this, too, for the one who is halted in
this halting of time, we have the perception of oneself as of one
person *too many*.

It is fascinating to note that, in Levinas's recent texts, the
same movement is sketched out, coming this time to be set not
in the word "shame," but in that of "bad conscience," where it
assumes its fully *ethical* meaning. This is a way of underscoring
afresh the secret continuity of the work, within which are real
discontinuities, as well as emphasizing all the promising wealth
of the 1935 essay.

A bad conscience: without intentions, without aims, under the
protective mask of the personage contemplating himself in the

mirror of the world, assured and positing himself. This conscious-ness is without a name, without situation, without titles. A pres-ence that dreads presence, naked of all attributes. . . . A bad con-science or a timidity: it is without acknowledged culpability and responsible for its own presence. Like the reserve of what is not in-vested, of the unjustified, or of the "stranger on the earth," ac-cording to the expression of the psalmist. This bad conscience is a reserve of the one without a fatherland, or of the one without a home who dares not enter. The interiority of mental life is, per-haps, originally this. It is not in the world, but in question. . . . To be qua bad conscience. This is to be in question but also unto the question; it is to have to respond . . . but consequently, in the af-firmation of its being as I, it has to respond for its right to be.[18]

So much for the description of the bad conscience. And now, for its being rooted in ethics, or in the relation to alterity:

To have to respond for one's right to be, not by reference to the abstraction of some anonymous law, of some juridical entity, but in the fear for another. Was not my "in the world" or my "place in the sun," and my home [*chez soi*] an usurpation of places that be-long to the other man, already oppressed by me, or hungry? This is a fear for all that my existing—despite its intentional and con-scious innocence—can accomplish of violence and murder. This is also a fear that goes back behind my "self-consciousness," and behind vicissitudes of pure persevering in being (whatever these may be), toward the good conscience. A fear that comes to me from the face of the other. It comes from the extreme uprightness of the face of the neighbor, tearing the plastic forms of the phe-nomenon. This is the uprightness of exposition to death, without defenses; and, before any language and any mimicry, a demand addressed to me from the depths of an absolute solitude; a de-mand addressed or an order signified, it is a putting in question of my presence and my responsibility.[19]

7. Yet again we find here the extreme proximity and extreme distance of anguish and nausea. The one and the other are essentially solitary phenomena, that is, they lay our essential solitude bare. The one and the other are phenomena whose ultimate sense and ontological significance are dissipated as soon as they are overcome in themselves. In this regard, as a counterpoint to Levinas's lines, we can read the following from Heidegger: "That anxiety reveals the nothing, man himself immediately demonstrates when anxiety has dissolved. In the lucid vision sustained by fresh remembrance we must say that that in the face of which and for which we were anxious was 'really'—nothing. Indeed: the nothing itself—as such—was there."[20]

Yet this should not hide from us that the *how* of this solitude is, in the one and the other case, essentially different. At the horizon of anxiety's solitude stands a man designated by a military metaphor as the lieutenant of being or of nothing, even if he were understood as a soldier-monk pushing his hermitry to the point of becoming a shepherd. The solitude of nausea has nothing of this haughty possibility; it points to a weakness, bearing down with the whole weight of the body exposed to its disease. It points to the weakness of him who, literally, is himself no longer *able*, but needs a hand in order to support his forehead so that he may vomit. What stands out on this horizon of nausea's solitude is a community, founded upon the maternity of tenderness or the fraternity of mutual aid.

8. Clearly we must pause at all these negative qualifications, repeated on this page (72; first page of §VII): impotence, imperfection, and finitude. What we must understand in the first place, and above all, is that all these qualifiers concern not

the *quid* [what] of being but its *quomodo* [in what way], the manner by which it gives itself in the relation that man maintains with it. Yet the finitude of being is not to be thought here on the basis of the meaning it takes in Heidegger, for whom being is finite because it is time and because it has "need of man in order to be" (see the French-language "Seminar of Thor," p. 306). The meaning of this finitude is here set on the basis of its two synonyms: impotence and imperfection. Impotence and imperfection designate the manner by which being posits itself: emphatically, to the point of imposing itself, to the point of nausea, even of being crushed in some sense or smothered under itself. However, in this way, impotence and imperfection are but the other aspect of infinitude, omnipotence, and perfection: it is *because* being posits itself "infinitely," *because* nothing can pose an obstacle to its omni-potence, *because* in its verbality "the fact of being is always already perfect"—that being is "finite," "essentially finite." *It is because in its* quid *it is this very power that in its* quomodo *it is this impotence.* In terms used later on, it is because being has the unstoppable insistence of the *there is* without respite that it is horror. But it is for this reason as well that, to a thinking that does not balk at "measuring without fear the whole weight of being and its universality," the watchword is: *escape.*

9. This reticence in regard to the idea of eternity, like the will underlying it to think time at once against Plato and against Heidegger, has been expressed in the very interesting review, published in *Recherches philosophiques* in 1934–1935, on a work today forgotten: *Total Presence* by Louis Lavelle.[21] What interested Levinas in this work was the rehabilitation of the *present*, as performed by Lavelle against the "German philoso-

phers" for whom "the flow of time laid out, in some sense, the opaque density of being: in the wake of a persistent, uneliminable past and before a future that is unknown but threatening, there was nothing but a fleeting present where nothing allowed us to catch our breath, or assert ourselves as our own masters." Yet the review ended nevertheless with an extremely interesting reticence, of which we cite the essentials:

The great merit of Mr. Lavelle consists in making us aware of this truth that the rehabilitation of the present is the sole means by which to break the tragic play of time. Yet for Mr. Lavelle, the victory over time is a stepping outside of time [*sortie en dehors du temps*]. Although the being that supports the subject might be pure act and in no way a substance, Mr. Lavelle's present is intemporal. It is the crossroads of time and eternity, but the promise of happiness is an arrow, sent off toward eternity. . . . Must the rehabilitation of the present—as apogee of time and a condition of freedom—lead us fatally to the encounter with that eternity so hard to separate from the impersonal coldness of a mathematical truth? Is Mr. Lavelle's present not a present eternity, stripped of the living wealth of the concrete present, rather than an eternal present wherein time itself furnishes the means to break the chains of the past? In other words, *is there not in time itself a perfection* other than the privilege of being a moving imitation of immobile eternity? [Rolland's emphasis]

A perfection of time outside any relation to the eternity whose "ontologistic character" *On Escape* had underscored (76); a perfection of time in itself against the essential "imperfection" of being. How could this not evoke for us, again, the late texts in which time finds that perfection of the otherwise than being, to be expressed as the beating of the Other in the Same and as *à-Dieu* [*to-God*].[22]

If nothing of this is effectively expressed in the 1935 essay, the preeminence [*précellence*] accorded to time over eternity nevertheless allows another trait of Levinas's thought to come through; it concretizes his effort to break with models of satisfaction, and was described recently as follows:

According to the models of satisfaction, the desire to possess commands the search, enjoyment is worth more than need, triumph is truer than failure, certitude is more perfect than doubt, and the answer goes farther than the question. Seeking, suffering, questioning would be simple diminutions of the happy find, of enjoyment, happiness, and the answer; insufficient thoughts of the identical and the present, indigent cognitions or cognition in the state of indigence. Once again this is good sense. This is also common sense.[23]

Here is an effort to break with the models of satisfaction that, inversely, signify that questioning, disquiet, desire, and time are *better* and signify *more* than answers, rest, satisfaction, or eternity. This is what another text, contemporary with the one just cited, states in a positive sense this time.

In the question—as in searching beyond the given—the Other disturbs the same an-archically, without being given as a presence (because, without giving itself [*sans se donner*]), without the absolute priority that would be a beginning and in which the Other would go back to a seeing that could only see in this Other another Same asserting itself in the eternity of being. The an-archy of the question and its rationality do not belong to the intrigue of knowledge and being, even though, in philosophy, this intrigue may be stated only in terms of knowledge and, thus stated, only to be contradicted. The question and its rationality do not belong to knowledge and being. This is so, even though Western philosophy represents an effort toward pacifying the question by the response, that is, an effort toward hearing the questioning as always bearing

on the given. Even though Western philosophy is an effort in view
of bringing to rest the dis-quiet always judged to be bad—even
when one calls it romantic—and in view of basing the given on a
foundation, which, moreover, amounts to conferring on it the essance of being.[24]

10. What we have just read can today, and to our mind
must, be understood as a rejection of the "problem of God"
such as it is posed in what we already are calling "onto-theo-
logy." (On this point, see Levinas's lectures on "God and Onto-
Theology" in *God, Death, and Time*, trans. Bettina Bergo [Stan-
ford, Calif.: Stanford University Press, 2000], pp. 121–24.) In
this sense—and however provocative such an assertion might
appear—Levinas should be understood as a thinker of the
"death of God." There then arises as a *problem* the maintenance
of the word "God," and, more than its simple "maintenance,"
the emphasis of its signification in Levinas's most mature
works, where it is thought as "*God not contaminated by being*"
(*Otherwise than Being*, p. xlii, underscored in the French text).
The maintenance of this term, and its emphasis even more, are
only possible through the renewal of the ancient problem of
God itself, conjoined with that of being. And the idea of creation can no longer be thought as the relationship of the
supreme Being to the rest of the beings that he grounds and
maintains in being, since God himself could no longer be
posited as a being but, precisely, signifies *beyond being, beyond
essance* or *otherwise than being*. If we could venture this expression, unfortunate in its sonority, we would have to say of God
that he "otherwise than is" [*autrement qu'est*]. For, this God signifies his passage only in the trace whereby he ordains me as
servant of that Other person [*d'Autrui*] whom he designates to
me as neighbor. But in so doing, the order of *justice* is estab-

lished—through the preoriginal intrigue of an an-archic subjectivity cut off from its good conscience or awakened as Other-within-the-Same—which is, in other words, the *justification of being* through what sometimes receives the name of *deaconry* [*diaconie*].

To be sure, if this bears repeating, the text on escape itself does not allow us to advance toward such audacious thoughts. Read "through the magic crystal," certain of its propositions do lead us to venture the hypothesis of the (if only latent) presence of such a problematic. And thus, we read: "The problem of the origin of being is not the problem of its proceeding out of nothingness, but that of its sufficiency or insufficiency. This problem is dictated by all that is revolting in the positing of being" (95). In the light cast by the "future of the free novel," we may translate the preceding in the following way. The problem of the origin of being that, when thought of as ess*a*nce, discloses its intimate affinity with the horrible and horrifying *there is*; this problem—which discloses what was, in those distant years, designated as being's insufficiency, its impotence, its imperfection, and its "finitude"—is the problem of being's justification by what is *better* than it, by the Good.

11. The value of European civilization is due not merely to its Greek origin—or to its being rooted in Greek ground, in which philosophy was born in dethroning "opinion, in which all tyrannies threaten and lay in wait"[25]—but also (above all?) to its Hebraic origin. This is indicated in other terms by "The Living Relevance of Maïmonides" [*L'actualité de Maïmonide*], a text contemporary with *On Escape*, published in 1935 in *Paix et Droit*.[26] We reproduce here its final sentences:

Paganism is not the negation of the spirit, nor the ignorance of a unique God. The mission of Judaism would be quite trivial if it limited itself to teaching monotheism to the earth's peoples. This would be to instruct those who already know. *Paganism is a radical powerlessness to get out of the world.* It consists not in denying spirits and gods but in situating them in the world. The Prime Mover, which Aristotle nevertheless isolated from the universe, was able to carry to the heights only the poor perfection of created things. Pagan morality is only the consequence of this basic incapacity to transgress the limits of the world. The pagan is shut up in this world, sufficient unto himself and closed upon himself. He finds it solid and firmly established. He finds it eternal. He orders his actions and his destiny according to the world. Israel's sentiment in regard to the world is entirely different. It is stamped by suspicion. The Jew does not have, in the world, the definitive foundations of the pagan. In the midst of the most complete confidence accorded to things, the Jew is tormented by a silent worry. As unshakable as the world might appear to those one calls healthy minds, it contains for the Jew the trace of the provisional and the created. This is the madness or the faith of Israel. Maimonides gave it a philosophical expression; he specified its true sense and its originality.

The value of Western civilization would thus be tied to its double origin, and principally to the call it receives from its Hebraic and biblical origin (whatever the permutations this call might have undergone in Christianity and its various forms, to the call to pass through the world rather than settling in it—in which we can hear: to go "beyond being." "For the little humanity that adorns the earth," according to the expression of the last page of *Otherwise than Being*, that page of breathless or panting beauty, for the little fraternity establishing humanity otherwise than as a pack of wolves—it will be necessary that the echo at least of this call still resound. This was an echo heard not by Odysseus but by Abraham, of the call of a Transcendence that has inscribed its trace not in the pre-Socratic fragments but in the rolls of the Torah.

Paganism, as the "acceptance of being" or as the "fundamental incapacity to transgress the limits of the world"—as the forgetting not of being but of the otherwise than being, or as a deafness to the call of a God "not contaminated by being"— would merit the name "barbarian" by leaving the field open to barbarism: in "accepting" being without *justifying* it. For its part, this justification is inseparable from ethics. We are reminded of this by the tamarind that Abraham planted at Beersheba (Genesis 21:32), which, according to the rabbinic interpretation, was not only a tree but first an acronym: "The three letters necessary to write its name in Hebrew are the initials of Nourishment, Drink, and Lodging, three things necessary to man, which man offers to man. The earth is for this. Man is its master in order to serve men."[27]

12. In order to close, we must come back one last time to this final sentence. How to understand the two expressions, "common sense" and "wisdom of the nations," with which it ends? Or rather, how shall we interpret these, for we would like to suggest nothing more than an interpretation here?

Let us therefore understand this "common sense" interpretively as the *good sense* that, as we know, is what is most commonly held on earth. Yet what the world thus shares superlatively is essentially the idea that being and meaning are united, more so than even the fingers of the hand, rather like the two sides of a coin. Thus this "common sense" must be understood precisely as "good sense" in the Cartesian sense of the term, that is, as reason and, more broadly, as thought—as thought thinking on its own scale, even when it deepens to the point of becoming the *thinking of the Same* (taking into account, here, the ambivalence of the genitive). A common sense as good sense, as reason, as thought thinking on its own scale, as the

thinking of the Same—or, again, as the "wisdom of the nations"! This is a wisdom in which the nations agree amongst
themselves [*s'entendent*], starting from Greece, to understand
[*entendre*] the identity of being and sense, or to understand
common sense. Could surpassing this "common sense" and this
"wisdom of the nations," could "getting out of being" in order
to understand or hear [*entendre*][28] a meaning "beyond being,"
be possible otherwise than by opening oneself to that wisdom
that, in the Bible, opposes the wisdom "of the nations"—i.e.,
that of Israel? Is this not what is suggested by these last lines in
the essay of 1935, and all the more so for us who read them
"through the magic crystal"?

Nevertheless, this does not mean deserting our "destinal
land," the *Abendland* [the West, or "evening land"], as the Hei-
deggerians will not fail to exclaim. It does not mean that we are
going astray in some middle East [*Orient moyen*] without so
much as venturing to the very end of the morning [*jusqu'à l'ex-
trème du matin*].[29] But what it perhaps signifies (which is this
time explicitly "anti-Heideggerian") is that this *Abendland* must
not be thought as determined only by its own morning, or by
the auroral words of Parmenides proclaiming the being-the-
same of being and thought [*l'être-le-même de l'être et de la pensée*]. But it also does not mean (and we can hardly say more
about this in these remarks, which, as we know, open more
problems than they resolve) that philosophy ought to return to
the status of the servant of religion (in one or another of its positive forms), nor the latter to the function of prop for the former. In this way, the whole problem of the relations between
religion and philosophy in Levinas is evoked—a problem that
should be elaborated on the basis of a remark like the following
one, at whose end we again find the words with which our introduction opened: "The biblical verses do not have as their

function to furnish proofs, but they bear witness to a tradition and an experience. Have they not a right to be quoted at least equal to that enjoyed by Hölderlin and Trakl? The question has a more general implication: have the Holy Scriptures, read and commented in the West, inflected or directed the Greek writings of the philosophers, or are they merely joined to these writings like a monstrosity? To philosophize: is this to decipher a hidden writing in a palimpsest?"[30]

[handwritten annotation:] esoteric writing

Notes

The text reprinted here ("Getting Out of Being by a New Path") appeared initially in volume 5 (1935–1936) of the *Recherches philosophiques*. In the present introduction, references to "On Escape" appear in parentheses after the citation and refer to the pagination of the present edition.

References provided in the notes without the name of the author all refer to the writings of E. Levinas. For the most frequently cited works, we have used the following abbreviations:

EE   *De l'existence à l'existant*, Paris: Editions de la Revue Fontaine, 1947. The work was republished from facsimiles in 1978 by the Librairie J. Vrin (Paris), with an unpaginated preface to which we refer as the preface to the second edition. English translation by Alphonso Lingis, *Existence and Existents* (Dordrecht and Boston: Nijhoff/ Kluwer Publishers, 1988); English pagination follows the original French pagination.

TO   *Le Temps et l'autre*, first published in *Le choix, le monde, l'existence*, ed. Jean Wahl (Paris: Arthaud, 1948). Reprinted by Fata Morgana (Montpellier, 1979). It is to the latter edition that we will refer. English translation by Richard A. Cohen, *Time and the Other and Additional Essays* (Pittsburgh, Penn.: Duquesne University Press, 1987); English pagination follows the French pagination.

TI   *Totalité et infini: Essai sur l'extériorité* (The Hague: Martinus Nijhoff, 1961). English translation by Alphonso Lingis,

Totality and Infinity: An Essay on Exteriority (Pittsburgh, Penn.: Duquesne University Press, 1969; The Hague: M. Nijhoff Publishers, 1979). Reprinted in 1998 by Duquesne University Press. English pagination follows the French pagination.

OB   *Autrement qu'être ou Au-delà de l'essence* (The Hague: Martinus Nijhoff, 1974). English translation by Alphonso Lingis, *Otherwise than Being or Beyond Essence* (The Hague: M. Nijhoff, 1981; Pittsburgh, Penn.: Duquesne University Press, 1998). English pagination follows the French pagination.

LETTER FROM EMMANUEL LEVINAS

1. *Recherches philosophiques*, Alexandre Koyré, Henri-Charles Puech, and Albert Spaier, eds. Six volumes of the journal appeared between 1931 and 1937. To the list of illustrious editors of the short-lived journal, we should add Henri-Charles Puech. [Levinas names the journal's editors in his letter to Rolland, although Wahl and Bachelard were not directly in charge of the journal. —Trans.]

GETTING OUT OF BEING BY A NEW PATH

1. Emmanuel Levinas, *L'humanisme de l'autre homme* (Montpellier: Fata Morgana, 1972).

2. Aleksandr Sergeevich Pushkin, *Eugene Onegin*, trans. Vladimir Nabokov (New York: Bollingen/Pantheon, 1964), p. 318.

Levinas evoked these verses of Pushkin during a conversation about *On Escape*. It is appropriate to point out here, notwithstanding, that this essay was written quite independently of M. Levinas.

[These last verses, which serve as a dénouement to this verse novel, read:

> Rushed by have many, many days
> since young Tatiana, and with her
> Onegin, in a blurry dream
> appeared to me for the first time—
> and the far stretch of a free novel

> I through a magic crystal
> still did not make out clearly.

—Trans.]

3. EE, preface to the second edition. [Levinas's preface to the second edition is not included in the English translation. —Trans.]

4. A movement altogether characteristic of Levinasian writing, which will appear above all in his great works and, no doubt most powerfully, in *OB*. This is a revolving movement that Silvano Petrosino defines in the following way: "Levinas's text *repeats itself*, but it is precisely in this repetition that it must be read. In this repetition, the writing does not progress, it deepens." See Silvano Petrosino and J. Rolland, *La vérité nomade* (Paris: Editions la Découverte, 1984).

5. This is the substantive "being," largely synonymous with "existence," which might be better rendered "to-be" if it were possible to nominalize "to-be." We avoid this, because later works of Levinas, including the lectures printed in *God, Death, and Time*, trans. Bettina Bergo (Stanford, Calif.: Stanford University Press, 2000), use "to-be" (e.g., *l'homme a à être*; man has to-be) in a highly specific way that concerns above all a different question in Heidegger. —Trans.

6. EE, preface to the second edition.

7. "Martin Heidegger and Ontology" in *Revue philosophique de la France et de l'étranger*, May–June 1932, pp. 395–431. It is this first version that we are using here, although the study was taken up again in an abridged form in *En découvrant l'existence avec Husserl et Heidegger* (Paris: Vrin, 1949, 2d enlarged edition, 1967). [*Discovering Existence with Husserl*, trans. Richard A. Cohen (Evanston, Ill.: Northwestern University Press, 1998). This translation omits the essays on Heidegger, which were translated into English by the Committee of Public Safety as "Emmanuel Levinas: Martin Heidegger and Ontology" in *Diacritics* 26, no. 1: pp. 11–32. —Trans.]

8. This is a debt explicitly recognized as such. We would take, by way of demonstration, OB, p. 49n28/189n28: "These lines and

those that follow owe much to Heidegger. Deformed and misunderstood? At least this deformation will not have been a way of denying the debt. Nor this debt a reason to forget." In the following year, Levinas's seminar on *Death and Time* spoke of "the debt of every contemporary researcher relative to Heidegger—a debt that he owes sometimes to his regret" (Jacques Rolland, Ed., *God, Death, and Time*, Bettina Bergo, trans., [Stanford, Calif.: Stanford University Press, 2001]. It was in regard to this remark that Jacques Derrida could say, in his eulogy to Emmanuel Levinas, on December 27, 1995: "The good fortune of our debt to Levinas is that we can, thanks to him, assume it and affirm it without regret, in a joyous innocence of admiration" (*Adieu: to Emmanuel Levinas*, Pascale-Anne Brault and Michael Nass, trans., [Stanford, Calif.: Stanford University Press, 1999], pp. 12–13). But this debt [*cela*], valid in his final years, was already at stake in 1935.

9. "Martin Heidegger et l'ontologie," see the unabridged version in the *Revue philosophique*, cited above, p. 414. [The sentence does not occur in the shortened version that appeared in the collection *En découvrant l'existence avec Husserl et Heidegger*. Neither does it appear in this form in the English translation by the Committee of Public Safety. —Trans.]

It is interesting to note that this comprehension already largely permeates Levinas's thesis on Husserl, published in 1930, *Théorie de l'intuition dans la phénoménologie de Husserl* (Paris: Librairie Académique Perrin, 1930; rpt. Librairie Philosophique J. Vrin, 1963), cf. pp. 14–15, 187–88, 217–18. [*The Theory of Intuition in the Phenomenology of Husserl*, trans. André Orianne (Evanston, Ill.: Northwestern University Press, 1973), pp. 11–13, 112–14, 149–51. —Trans.]

10. To avoid any ambiguity, recall that the couple existence-existent is, for Levinas, the equivalent of that of being-beings. He will put this clearly, moreover, in the following way: "Let us come back to Heidegger. You are not unaware of his distinction . . . between *Sein* and *Seiendes*, being and beings, which I prefer to translate, for reasons of pronunciation [*euphonie*], 'existing' and 'existent,' without lending a specifically existentialist sense to these terms." See TO, p. 24/44.

11. "Martin Heidegger et l'ontologie," p. 402; English translation, p. 17. It is worth noting here that virtually all of Levinas's books begin by recalling, in various forms, the ontological difference. See therefore EE, p. 15/17; TI, p. 13/42–43; OB, p. ix/xli.

12. See *Noms propres* (Montpellier: Fata Morgana, 1976), p. 9. [*Proper Names*, trans. Michael B. Smith (Stanford, Calif.: Stanford University Press, 1996), p. 3 (translation modified for fluency with the French). —Trans.]

13. "Martin Heidegger et l'ontologie," unabridged version in the *Revue philosophique* cited above, p. 407. The sentence does not occur in the shortened version that appeared in the collection *En découvrant l'existence avec Husserl et Heidegger*. We should note by contrast that theoreticism—the fact that "theory or representation plays a preponderant role in life; it serves as the basis of all conscious life; it is that form of intentionality, which assures the foundation of all the others" (*Theory of Intuition*, p. 86/53)—is the point on which Levinas will diverge from Husserl over the whole course of the former's life. This is the case even though, as Jacques Derrida notes, Levinas was "very attentive to all that which tempers or complicates the primordiality of theoretical consciousness in Husserl's analyses" [*Writing and Difference*, p. 128/87, translation modified for fluency with the text].

14. [Happiness in being will be discussed subsequently in *Totality and Infinity*, in light of "love of life," which makes the escape of the early concept "excendance" into the "transcendance" of the mature work, TI. See TI, p. 35. —Trans.]

15. EE, p. 19/19. [Translation modified for fluency with the text. —Trans.]

16. This is a remark that constitutes not so much a "critique" as, if we may nonetheless venture this word in regard to him who gave it its meaning, a situation of Heidegger's thought, for which the expression "getting out of being" can only sound like pure nonsense. And here, no doubt, we touch upon the radical and perhaps necessary incomprehension between these two thinkers. This is an incomprehension that must, in an initial moment, be understood on the basis of what Heidegger notes about the thinkers of metaphysics: "The great thinkers never understand one another

fundamentally, precisely because on each occasion they desire the Same, in the figure of the grandeur proper to them. If they desired something different, then comprehension, that is, tolerance, would not be so difficult." See Heidegger, *Schelling*, trans. Jean-François Courtine (Paris: Gallimard, 1977), pp. 32–33. [*Schelling's Treatise on the Essence of Human Freedom*, trans. Joan Stambaugh (Athens: Ohio University Press, 1985); translation modified for fluency with the French. —Trans.]

This, however, is an incomprehension that, in a second instant, designates an entirely other difference, in the sense that Heidegger is no longer he who desires the Same, interpreted as a foundation according to one or another historical figure. He is rather the philosopher who *thinks* the Same precisely as the historiality of being, that is, of being that is susceptible to presenting itself in diverse figures, whereas Levinas *thinks* the Same, structured as the ontological difference, as incapable of silencing another question, which is the question of the Other [*l'Autre*], coming to pass in the form of the Other person [*Autrui*], the other man and the Infinite. Consequently, we must admit here that what impedes comprehension and tolerance is ultimately that Heidegger and Levinas, in this sense, *do not think the Same*. Yet we should perhaps see in this a sign that the omnipotence of the Same finds its limit with this other question which, desiring to smother the latter by ejecting Levinas from the field of thought toward a "religious discourse," did little else in effect than to accuse of rabies the dog it sought to drown [*accuser de la rage le chien qu'il veut seulement noyer*].

17. The expression *there is* [*il y a*] is used without reference to the precise meaning it will take on in the later Levinas, which we will evoke in the pages to come.

18. In his examination of the "existential constitution of the "There," Heidegger defines *Geworfenheit* ["thrownness"]. Thus, he writes:

> What we indicate *ontologically* by the term "state-of-mind" is *ontically* the most familiar and everyday sort of thing; our mood, our Being-attuned. . . . In having a mood, *Dasein* is

always disclosed moodwise as that entity to which it has been delivered over in its Being; and in this way it has been delivered over to the Being which, in existing, it has to be. . . . This characteristic of *Dasein*'s Being—this "that it is"—is unveiled in its "whence" and "whither," yet disclosed in itself all the more unveiledly; we call it the "*thrownness*" of this entity into its "there"; indeed, it is thrown in such a way that, as Being-in-the-world, it is the "there."

Heidegger, *Being and Time*, trans. John Macquarrie and Edward Robinson (New York: Harper and Row, 1962), ¶ 29, pp. 172–74. Later he adds, "Thrownness is neither a 'fact that is finished' nor a Fact that is settled. *Dasein*'s facticity is such that *as long as* it is what it is, *Dasein* remains in the throw, and is sucked into the turbulence of the 'they''s inauthenticity. Thrownness, in which facticity lets itself be seen phenomenally, belongs to *Dasein*, for which, in its Being, that very Being is an issue" (¶ 38, p. 223). —Trans.

19. This is how Levinas translates Heidegger's term *Dasein*, or being-there, in this study.

[Note, however, that Levinas's use of the term "ici-bas" (rather than simply "ici" or "là") to translate the German *da-*, generally rendered in English by "there," enriches this "there" in a useful way. The French "ici-bas" literally means "here below" or "here on earth," and so, obliquely, it refers both to the human world and to what defines it as "here below," i.e., the sky or the heavens. Levinas's intention is clearly to suggest by "ici-bas" the world in which *Dasein* finds itself and for which it feels concern. —Trans.]

20. "Martin Heidegger and Ontology," pp. 416–17. [I have modified this translation, in a few places, to bring it closer to Rolland's reproduction. —Trans.]

Levinas has explicitly compared this approach to existence with Heidegger's notion of "thrownness" (*Geworfenheit*), writing:

I do not believe that Heidegger could allow an existing without an existent, which would seem absurd to him. Nevertheless, he has a notion, *Geworfenheit*, that is generally translated as "dereliction" or "desertion." Emphasis is thereby laid upon a consequence of *Geworfenheit*. We should translate *Geworfenheit* by the "fact-of-being-thrown-into" . . . existence. It is as though the existent only appeared in an existence that preceded it, as though existence were independent of the existent, and as though the existent that finds itself thrown therein could never become the master of existence. It is precisely for this reason that there is desertion and abandonment. Thus dawns the idea of an existing that occurs [*se fait*] without us, without a subject, of an existing without an existent.

TO, pp. 24–25/45 [translation modified for fluency with the French].

21. "Martin Heidegger and Ontology," p. 417. [Of this "projecting" or *Entwurf*, Heidegger writes in *Being and Time*, ¶ 31, "Being-There as Understanding":

> Why does the understanding—whatever may be the essential dimensions of that which can be disclosed in it—always press forward into possibilities? It is because the understanding has in itself the existential structure that we call "projection" [*Entwurf*]. With equal primordiality the understanding projects *Dasein*'s Being both upon its "for-the-sake-of-which" and upon significance, as the worldhood of its current world. The character of understanding as projection is constitutive for Being-in-the-world. . . . And as thrown, *Dasein* is thrown into the kind of Being which we call "projecting." Projecting has nothing to do with comporting oneself towards a plan that has been thought out, and in accordance with which *Dasein* arranges its Being. On the contrary, any *Dasein* has, as *Dasein*, already projected itself; and as long as it is, it is projecting.
>
>   Translation modified. —Trans.]

22. The notion is originally from Heidegger; see his *Ontology: The Hermeneutic of Facticity*, trans. John Van Buren (Bloomington: Indiana University Press, 1999). —Trans.

23. We cite the new translation by Roger Munier in *Cahiers de l'Herne*, no. 45 (1983). Parenthetical references in the following citations are as follows: *Was ist Metaphysik?* (Frankfurt am Main: Vittorio Klostermann, 1969) / Roger Munier's translation noted above / Henry Corbin's translation, published in *Heidegger: Questions I* (Paris: Gallimard, 1968). [See "What Is Metaphysics?" ed. and trans. David Farrell Krell, in *Basic Writings: From 'Being and Time' (1927) to 'The Task of Thinking' (1964)* (New York: Harper and Row, 1977), pp. 95–116. —Trans.]

24. There is here, in the use and the enrichment of the same word in very close senses by Sartre and Levinas, a case of a philosophical encounter all the more interesting because we cannot speak of an influence in either direction.

In effect, "On Escape" appeared three years before the publication of *Nausea*. But, even if we might suppose that Sartre was a reader of the journal *Recherches philosophiques*, we cannot overlook the fact that the very first version of Sartre's novel goes back to 1931; neither can we ignore that the title was Gaston Gallimard's find, to which Sartre only grudgingly consented.

25. The last stanza of Rimbaud's "Les assis" [The Seated Ones] reads:

> Puis ils ont une main invisible qui tue:
> Au retour, leur regard filtre ce venin noir
> Qui charge l'oeil souffrant de la chienne battue,
> Et vous suez, pris dans un atroce entonnoir!

> And they have an invisible hand that kills:
> Upon return, their gaze filters this black venom
> That fills the suffering eye of the beaten bitch,
> And you sweat, caught in an atrocious funnel!

This is one of his famous satires of his life in the town of Charleville, dated 1871. The best known of these poems is "Le cœur volé" [The Stolen Heart]. "Les assis" presents the pallid horror of the habitués of the reading-room. See John Porter Houston, *The Design of Rimbaud's Poetry* (New Haven, Conn.: Yale University Press, 1963). Also see EE's citation from "Les assis," p. 26. —Trans.

26. For Heidegger, the "Stimmung" or mood, or "state of mind," refers to "existential" determinations. That is, the mood has a psychological or everyday definition, but *what it is capable of revealing to us* about ourselves as being-there, is "not [the] property of something present-at-hand, but essentially existential ways to be." For example, he writes, "The pallid, evenly balanced lack of mood [*Ungestimmtheit*], which is often persistent and which is not to be mistaken for a bad mood, is far from nothing at all. Rather, it is in this that *Dasein* becomes satiated with itself. Being has become manifest as a burden. Why that should be, one does not *know*" (*Being and Time*, ¶ 29). Mood thus reveals to a *Dasein* that which objective knowledge, or objectifying intentionality cannot reveal. —Trans.

27. Note that, in French, "upset stomach," "heartburn," or feeling "sick at heart" are called *mal au cœur*, just as "seasickness" is also conceived as a "*mal*," *mal de mer*. The English "sickness" or "ills" do not have the same conceptual extension as the French *mal*, which, adjectivally, functions for physiological, moral, and aesthetic situations. —Trans.

28. Let us note that the movement of Mallarmé's poem "Brise marine" [Sea Breeze] is the inverse of that, here, from which we borrow some of his elements.

[Mallarmé wrote this early poem at age twenty-two (1964, collected in *From Contemporary Parnassus*). The stanza Rolland cites illustrates the desire for escape. It reads:

> How sad the flesh! And there's no more to read.
> Escape, far off! I feel that somewhere birds
> Are drunk to be amid strange spray and skies!
> Nothing, not those old gardens eyes reflect
> Can now restrain this heart steeped in the sea
> Oh nights! Nor the lone brightness of my lamp
> On the blank paper which its whiteness shields
> Nor the young wife, her baby at her breast.
> I shall depart! Steamer with swaying masts,
> Raise anchor for exotic wilderness!

In Mary Ann Caws, ed., *Stéphane Mallarmé: Selected Poetry and Prose* (New York: New Directions, 1982), p. 16. —Trans.]

29. Feeling, whose very manner of being refers us to the philosophy of Merleau-Ponty. We note, moreover, in this regard, that Merleau-Ponty's theses on perception are discussed in Levinas's *Signification et sens*, reprinted in his *Humanisme de l'autre homme* (Montpellier: Fata Morgana, 1972). ["Meaning and Sense," in *Emmanuel Levinas: Collected Philosophical Papers*, trans. Alphonso Lingis, with notes by Adriaan Peperzak (Dordrecht: Martinus Nijhoff, 1987), pp. 75–105. —Trans.]

30. We are here picking up Henry Corbin's translation in *Questions I.* Roger Munier translates *wir schweben* as "we are in suspense" [*nous sommes en suspens*].

31. Rolland cites Munier's translation of *Was ist Metaphysik?* here: "Un malaise nous gagne." —Trans.

32. Rolland cites Henry Corbin's translation, *Qu'est-ce que la métaphysique?*: "On se sent oppressé." —Trans.

33. Here Rolland emphasizes the meaning of *dépaysé* by hyphenating it. *Dépaysé* literally means "un-homed," "taken out of one's country." —Trans.

34. "Le rien" is Levinas's translation of Heidegger's *das Nichts*, and precedes Sartre's *le néant*—which is inspired from the same Heideggerian term, and which English translations have rendered "nothingness." I will use both "nothingness" and occasionally "nothing" to maintain a contemporary tone in the translation, for though "the nothing" is a somewhat better translation (since "nothing-*ness*" intensifies the substantialization of "nothing," which is not useful), it has an anachronistic overtone. See Heidegger, *Being and Time*, ⁋ 58, and "What Is Metaphysics?" pp. 95–116.

The latter defines it thus:

> The nothing reveals itself in anxiety—but not as a being. Just as little is it given as an object. Anxiety is no kind of grasping of the nothing. All the same, the nothing reveals itself in and through anxiety, although, to repeat, not in such

a way that the nothing becomes manifest in our malaise quite apart from beings as a whole. Rather we said that in anxiety the nothing is encountered at one with beings. . . . This wholly repelling gesture toward beings that oppresses *Dasein* in anxiety is the essence of the nothing: nihilation (pp. 104–105).

—Trans.

35. See Martin Heidegger, *Zeit und Sein*, text with French translation by F. Fédier in *L'endurance de la pensée* (Paris: Plon, 1968), pp. 38–39. [*On Time and Being*, trans. Joan Stambaugh (New York: Harper and Row, 1972). —Trans.]

36. Levinas, TI, p. 165/190 [translation modified for consistency with the French —Trans.], Rolland's emphasis.

37. EE, p. 93/57.

38. This expression is also used by Levinas in his essay "Signature," in *Difficile liberté* (Paris: Albin Michel, 1976, 2d ed.), p. 375. [*Difficult Freedom: Essays on Judaism*, trans. Seán Hand (Baltimore, Md.: Johns Hopkins University Press, 1990), p. 292. —Trans.]

39. EE, p. 94/58.

40. TA, pp. 25–26/46–47. [Translation modified for fluency with the French. —Trans.]

41. Maurice Blanchot, "Notre companion clandestine," in *Textes pour Emmanuel Lévinas* (Paris: Jean-Michel Place, 1980), p. 86. ["Our Clandestine Companion," in Richard A. Cohen, trans. and ed., *Face to Face with Levinas* (Albany: State University of New York Press, 1985), pp. 41–50. —Trans.]

42. This is what I have attempted to show in my study on the *neuter* in Blanchot. See *Exercises de la patience*, no. 2 (Winter 1981), pp. 11–45.

43. Blanchot, *L'espace littéraire* (Paris: Gallimard, 1968), pp. 215–16. [English translation by Ann Smock, "The Outside, the Night," in *The Space of Literature* (Lincoln: University of Nebraska Press, 1982), p. 163. —Trans.]

This reference to Blanchot does not appear random to us, for at least two reasons. The first reason is tied to the fact, already noted, that the Blanchotian neuter only seems thinkable in its relation to Levinas's *there is*. The second, and thinner, reason is due to the rather astonishing fact that Blanchot used the term *there is* in a short story that he wrote while Levinas was drafting "On Escape" ("Le dernier mot" [The Last Word] in Blanchot, *Le ressassement éternel* [Paris: Minuit, 1951, 1983]). Indeed, Blanchot used the term in a sense that must clearly be brought together with the one we are analyzing here. However, we can only cite this text here, though it would merit a word-for-word analysis:

> I ran away. It was already dusk. The city was invaded by smoke and clouds. Only the doors of the houses were visible, barred with gigantic inscriptions. A cold dampness was shining on the cobblestones. When I went down the stairway beside the river, some large dogs appeared on the opposite bank. They were similar to mastiffs and their heads bristled with crowns of thorns. I knew that the justice department [*la justice*] used these dogs from time to time and that they had been trained to be quite ferocious. But I belonged to the justice department as well [*j'appartenais à la justice*]. That was my shame: I was a judge. Who could condemn me? Instead of filling the night with their barking, the dogs silently let me pass, as though they had not seen me. It was only after I had walked some distance that they began to howl again: trembling, muffled howls, which at that hour of the day resounded like the echo of the words *there is*.
>
> "That, no doubt, is the last word," I thought, listening to them.
>
> But the word *there is* was nevertheless enough to reveal the things in this distant quarter, before reaching the villa, I entered a real garden with trees, roots tangled along the ground, a whole thicket of branches and plants . . ."

Maurice Blanchot, "The Last Word," trans. Paul Auster, in *Vicious Circles: Two Fictions and "After the Fact"* (Barrytown, N.Y.: Station Hill Press, 1985), p. 45.

44. EE, preface to the second edition. [This preface is not reproduced in the English translation. Comparable remarks on the

"there is" are found in chapter 1, "Introduction: The Existent and the Relationship with Existence," pp. 17–20. —Trans.]

45. The abandonment of the stratagem of the feint underscores its Cartesian character, and makes it comparable to the strategy of the hyperbolic doubt. See the final pages of Descartes's *First Meditation.*

[As Descartes expressed it: "It is now some years since I detected how many were the false beliefs that I had from my earliest youth admitted as true; and from that time I was convinced that I must once and for all seriously undertake to rid myself of all the opinions which I had formerly accepted, and commence to build anew." *Discourse on the Method and Meditations on First Philosophy,* ed. David Weissman (New Haven, Conn.: Yale University Press, 1996), p. 58. —Trans.]

46. And, among these pages, we note the very first, where we read the following. "Being's *esse* dominates not-being [*le ne-pas-être*] itself." See OB, p. 3/3.

47. OB, p. ix/xli, translation modified for fluency with the French and to preserve the metaphor of the musical note. —Trans.

48. Ibid. —Trans.

49. See "De la déficience sans souci au sens nouveau," in *Concilium,* no. 113 (March 1976). Reprinted in *De Dieu qui vient à l'idée* (Paris: Vrin, 1982), p. 78n1. ["From the Carefree Deficiency to the New Meaning," in *Of God Who Comes to Mind,* trans. Bettina Bergo (Stanford, Calif.: Stanford University Press, 1996), p. 195n1. —Trans.]

50. OB, pp. 207–208/163. [Translation corrected, as the English translation omits the crucial words "fail to" (*ne peut pas ne pas*) —Trans.]

51. OB, p. 49/38.

52. This text is now available from the publisher, Editions Rivages (Paris, 1997). It is followed by an important essay by Miguel Abensour, whose merit is to have laid out its philosophical range and implications, situating it in relation to "On Escape." ["Reflections on Hitlerism," trans. Seán Hand, *Critical Inquiry* 17, no. 1 (Autumn 1990), 62–71. —Trans.]

53. "Reflections on Hitlerism," p. 71.

54. Ibid., p. 67, emphasis added.

55. TO, 55/69.

56. "Reflections on Hitlerism," p. 68.

57. Ibid., p. 69.

58. Ibid., p. 70.

59. Léon Poliakov, *Le bréviaire de la haine* (Paris: Calmann-Lévy, 1951), p. 2. [*Harvest of Hate: The Nazi Program for the Destruction of the Jews of Europe* (forward by Reinhold Niebuhr) (New York: Holocaust Library, Schocken Books, 1979), p. 2. —Trans.]

60. "Reflections on Hitlerism," p. 70.

61. Raul Hilberg, *La destruction des juifs d'Europe*, trans. A. Charpentier and M.-F. de Paloméra (Paris: Fayard, 1988), p. 901. [*The Destruction of the European Jews* (New York: Holmes and Meier, 1985), p. 1044. —Trans.]

62. Blanchot, *L'entretien infini* (Paris: Gallimard, 1969), p. 63. [*The Infinite Conversation*, trans. Susan Hanson, (Minneapolis: University of Minnesota Press, 1993), p. 44. —Trans.] This idea of suffering as *lost time* is also expressed, in a very strong way, in Blanchot's narrative *Le dernier homme* (Paris: Gallimard, 1957), pp. 98–99. We transcribe the following passage from that work:

> "I think I could die, but not suffer—no, I can't." "Are you afraid of suffering?" She shivered. "I'm not afraid of it, I just can't, I can't." An answer which at the time only seemed to me to contain a reasonable fear, but perhaps she had meant something quite different, perhaps at that moment she had expressed the reality of the suffering one could not suffer, and perhaps she had thereby revealed one of her most secret thoughts: that she, too, would have been dead a long time ago—so many people had died around her—if, in order to die, one had not had to pass through such a thickness of sufferings that were not fatal and if she had not been terrified of losing her way in an area of pain so dark that she would never find the way out.

[*The Last Man*, trans. Lydia Davis (New York: Columbia University Press, 1987), p. 55. —Trans.]

63. TO, 59/71.

64. The French "du moi à soi-même" reads literally, "of the me to oneself." A few lines farther, Levinas adds, "It is therefore our intimacy, that is, *our presence to ourselves* [notre présence à nous-mêmes]." In the first instance, it is not my presence to *my*-self [moi-*même*] that is in question, the *soi-* of *soi-même* is not posited as our identity or our ego or our *moi*. Our *soi-même* is paradoxically material—though not the way a thing or a body is material; it is material in the way *exposure* and vulnerability is 'material,' i.e., open to being touched or harmed, or ashamed. It is experienced through sensation and affect (nausea and shame) rather than reflectively. And in the moment of being experienced, it is not reflected in an idealist sense as I-am-I. Yet *soi-même* is also not an object. Hence Levinas can mean the same thing when he writes "presence of the ego to *it*self" and "our presence to *our*selves." In the later work *Otherwise than Being or Beyond Essence*, Levinas will write:

> What we are here calling oneself [*soi-même*], or the other in the same, where inspiration arouses respiration, . . . precedes this empirical order, which is part of being, of the universe, of the State. . . . Here we are trying to express the unconditionality of a subject, which does not have the status of a principle. . . . The self is a *sub-iectum*; it is under the weight of the universe. . . . To be in-oneself, backed up against oneself . . . is for the I to be in itself, lying in itself beyond essence.

OB, p. 147/116. —Trans.

65. We cannot fail to admire Masaccio's fresco *Adam and Eve Driven Out of Paradise*, in the Brancacci Chapel of the Church of the Carmines, in Florence. The one and the other figure are naked, which contradicts the biblical text (Genesis 3:21), in which it says that the Eternal clothed them with animal skin tunics. Both are naked and walking toward the accursed earth. Yet, while Eve raises toward the sky a face with closed eyes and features twisted by pain, Adam, his shoulders bent forward, hides his face with his hands. Although he and his companion sewed loin cloths from fig leaves, when they found their eyes had been opened, Adam thought of hiding not his sex but rather his face.

If we think, from "On Escape" forward in time, of what the face will become in Levinas's later writings, and in *Totality and Infinity* in particular, we find ourselves wondering whether, in Adam's gesture, beyond his body it is the patency, the *too visible quality of his being* that Adam is trying to hide. In that case, Masaccio represented his nakedness "by mistake," in order to show Adam's "need to exonerate for his existence."

66. Two remarks are worth making here. The patricide is carried out here without remorse, and it will be repeated just after the War: "The dialectic these developments may contain is in any case not Hegelian. It is not a matter of traversing a series of contradictions, or of reconciling them while stopping history. On the contrary, it is toward a pluralism that does not merge into unity that I should like to make my way and, if this can be dared, to break with Parmenides." TO, 20/42. Note, moreover, that the philosophical aim of Levinas's late seminar, "Death and Time," is to arrive at a concept of pure nothingness that is not already indebted to being and which, as such, might reach the excess of death.

67. EE, preface to the second edition [only in the French].

68. EE, p. 111/66.

69. TO, p. 31/52.

70. EE, p. 121/71 [Translation modified for fluency with the text. —Trans.], Rolland's emphasis.

71. TI, p. 165/191. [Lingis translates *sortie de* as "deliverance from." —Trans.]

72. The second section of *Totality and Infinity* is entitled "Interiority and Economy." It works out an extensive phenomenology of enjoyment as love of life, the creation of a dwelling through labor, and the work of language and representation. —Trans.

73. TI, p. 92/119–20. [Translation modified.]

74. It was Jean-Luc Marion who, in his work *The Idol and Distance: Five Studies* (trans. Thomas Carlson [New York: Fordham University Press, 2001]), showed irrefutably how *Totality and Infinity* proceeded to a (simple) inversion of the terms of the ontological difference and, thereby, remained prisoner to that difference. He subsequently returned to this question to reconsider

it (see his "Note sur l'indifférence ontologique" ["A Note Concerning the Ontological Indifference," trans. Jeffrey L. Kosky, *Graduate Faculty Philosophy Journal* 20, no. 2 and 21, no. 1 (1998)]) and to show how *Otherwise than Being,* which *The Idol and Distance* ignored confidently, no longer functioned according to this logic of inversion and, to that degree, gave itself the wherewithal to "let significations from beyond the ontological difference signify." Also see remarks I made, with Silvano Petrosino, on this question, but before Marion's reconsideration, in *La verité nomade*, pp. 100–102.

75. EE, preface to the second edition, Rolland's emphasis. —Trans.

76. TI, p. 6/36 for all three citations.

77. OB, p. x/xli [translation modified for fidelity to the French text and its innovations].

78. "The I [*moi*] is the very crisis of the being of beings within the human sphere [*de l'être de l'étant dans l'humain*]." "Ethique comme philosophie première," *Le Nouveau Commerce* 84–85, p. 19.

79. The French text reads, "expulsion par l'Autre s'installant pour y battre au cœur du Même." —Trans.

80. OB, p. 67/52. [Translation modified.]

81. Blanchot, *L'espace littéraire*, preliminary note. [The note discusses the meaning of the center: "A book, even fragmentary, has a center that attracts it: a center not fixed, but one that is displaced by the pressure of the book and the circumstances of its composition." —Trans.]

82. OB, 209/164 [translation modified for fluency with the French]. One parallel with *De l'évasion* is seen immediately in the hyphenation of "dis-heartening," or *é-cœurant*, which means sickening more readily than it means disheartening [compare the French *mal au cœur* for nausea, which Levinas and Rolland discuss. —Trans.].

83. This expression is proposed in EE, preface to the second edition. But the "spatial metaphor" is never simple in Levinas, where it never goes without posing a question, as Derrida had noted in 1968, in regard to height.

Inaccessible, the invisible is the most-high. This expression—
inhabited perhaps by the Platonic resonances Levinas evokes,
but above all by others that we recognize more readily—tears
apart the spatial inscription of the metaphor by its superlative excess. However high it may be, height is always acces-
sible. The most-high is higher than height. No increase of
height could measure it. The most-high does not belong to
space, it is not of this world. But what is the necessity of this
inscription of language in space at the very moment at
which it [the most-high] exceeds it [language]?

Derrida, *Writing and Difference*, p. 139/93; also see p. 149/100–101.

84. OB, p. 209/164. [Translation modified for fluency with the
French. —Trans.]

85. OB, p. 3/3. Also see "Hermeneutics and Beyond" in *Of
God Who Comes to Mind*, p. 172/110. Levinas asks there, "But can a
hermeneutics of the religious do without unbalanced thoughts [*pen-
sées déséquilibrées*]? And does philosophy itself not consist in treat-
ing 'mad' thoughts with wisdom or in bringing wisdom to love?"

86. See, in regard to such language, the illuminating remark in
the final version of Levinas's "Signature" [in *Difficult Freedom: Essays on Judaism*]: "It has been possible to present, since *Totality
and Infinity*, this relation with the Infinite as irreducible to 'thema-
tization.' . . . The *ontological language*, which *Totality and Infinity
still uses* in order to exclude the purely psychological significance of
the proposed analyses, *is henceforth avoided*. And the analyses
themselves refer not to the *experience* in which a subject always
thematizes what he equals, but to the *transcendence* in which he
answers for that which his intentions have not encompassed" [p.
397/295; Rolland's emphasis except for the last sentence. —Trans.].
It seemed to us possible to affirm that it is thanks alone to the
abandonment of the ontological language that the analyses have
been able to pass from experience to transcendence. In this way,
the manner or turn of thinking that was invented in *Otherwise
than Being* is indissociable from the manner or turn of writing by
which it is expressed.

87. "This century will thus have been, for everyone, the end of

philosophy!" exclaimed Levinas in 1956 (cf. "On Maurice Blanchot," in *Proper Names*, trans. Michael B. Smith [Stanford, Calif.: Stanford University Press, 1996], p. 127; translation modified). For everyone, perhaps, but not for him who will have held this name [philosophy] with an attitude that it would be a fundamental error to consider conservative. By way of demonstration, I cite the last words of a conversation Levinas had with Richard Kearney:

> It is true that philosophy, in its traditional form as onto-theology and logocentrism—to use terms from Heidegger and Derrida—has reached a limit. But it is not true in the sense of philosophical speculation and critical questioning. The speculative exercises of philosophy are in no sense ready to end. In effect, the entire contemporary discourse on metaphysics is much more speculative than metaphysics itself. Reason is never more volatile than when it places itself in question. In the contemporary end of philosophy, philosophy has found its own vitality.

Richard Kearney, *Dialogues with Contemporary Continental Thinkers: The Phenomenological Heritage. Paul Ricoeur, Emmanuel Levinas, Herbert Marcuse, Stanislas Breton, Jacques Derrida* (Manchester: Manchester University Press, 1984).

ON ESCAPE

1. Levinas ends the sentence with an ellipsis to indicate that the ongoing concern of philosophy with transcendence will be interrupted, here, historically and, as it were, syntactically. The beginning of the following paragraph announces the interruption, which is none other than the possible end of discourses on infinite being, brought about by the "modern sensibility" in philosophy and elsewhere. —Trans.

2. The substantive *inamovibilité* is one of several metaphors used by Levinas that are borrowed from a juridical vocabulary. The term refers precisely to the quality of certain magistrates and judges, who can be neither displaced from, nor deprived of, their functions without exceptional procedures. —Trans.

3. In the original text the verbs "fix" and "create" are in the plural; they are the actions of both the vital urge and the creative becoming. The French permits an *inclusive* disjunction (either a, or b, or both) with the use of the conjunction "ou", thus: "l'élan vital ou le devenir créateur, qui . . . ne se fixent nullement d'avance leur terme . . . " —Trans.

4. The word is modeled upon "trans-scendence," adjoining "ex-" or "out" to the Latin *scandere*, "to climb". —Trans.

5. The usual French formulation is *dans cette référence à lui-même, l'homme* ["in this reference to himself, man . . . "], but here Levinas is emphasizing the *one-self*, such that the phrase should read literally: "in this reference to oneself, man . . . " The oneself refers to the self of fatigue, sensibility, affectivity, which accompanies our reflective consciousness sometimes like a weight. Levinas develops this theme in 1940 in EE. The *soi-même* receives emphasis as vulnerability and suffering in OB. —Trans.

6. Levinas deliberately writes *caractère ontologiste* here, and not *caractère ontologique*. "Ontologiste" is an adjective carrying a certain irony, which could be translated as relative-to-ontology or ontologies, rather than relative to being or existence. This is an oblique reference to Heidegger's discussion of nothing [*Nichts*]; see *Being and Time*, § 40, pp. 228–35 and § 57, pp. 319–25. —Trans.

7. By dint of the play of gendered articles, Levinas here creates a sort of pun that reads both as: "Prudish modesty [*elle*] does not leave need [*il, le*] once the latter is satisfied" *and* as: "She does not leave him when he is satisfied." This is all the more comical since we are talking about the endurance of modesty in the intimacy of nakedness. —Trans.

8. Sartre's novel by this title first appeared in December 1938, published by Gallimard. The present essay dates from 1935. Also see the remarks in EE on nausea contrasted with horror (p. 96/61). —Trans.

9. The French text reads: "Elle ne saurait qu'être foncièrement étrangère au plan même où une volonté peut se heurter à des obstacles ou subir une tyrannie. Car elle est la marque de l'existence de l'existant." The feminine pronoun "elle" appears to refer to the

brutality of existence ("la brutalité de l'existence," both nouns being feminine). Ambiguity arises because in the previous sentence "limitation" is also a feminine noun, and it is typical of *human* existence to encounter obstacles and limitations. But given what preceded this, brutality is, for Levinas, the proper mark of *existence itself,* or of being, because by essence "being is finite" and a "burden to itself" in its powerlessness. —Trans.

10. The French reads: "Placer derrière l'être le créateur, conçu à son tour comme un être, ce n'est pas non plus poser le commencement de l'être en dehors des conditions de l'être déjà constitué." Levinas is enumerating two cases where the problem of origin is highlighted by the contradiction implicit in defining the beginning of being—whether as event or as creation—as a function of a preexisting cause or of some being that preexists the emergence of being itself. He is looking, as he will say, for a paradox rather than a contradiction. The paradox is illuminated by the phenomenon of nausea, where being, which is always already weighty or grave, becomes oppressed by itself, smothers in itself. —Trans.

11. Henri Bergson, *Creative Evolution,* "The Idea of 'Nothing,'" trans. Arthur Mitchell (Westport, Conn.: Greenwood Press, 1975). In this chapter, first published separately in the *Revue philosophique* (November 1906), Bergson offers what will later be, for Levinas, one path of criticism of Heidegger's philosophy of being. Bergson writes, "Existence appears to me like a conquest over naught [nothingness]. I say to myself that there might be, that indeed there ought to be, nothing, and I then wonder that there is something. Or I represent all reality extended on nothing as on a carpet: at first it was nothing, and being has come to superaddition to it. Or, yet again, if something has always existed, nothing must always have served as its substratum or receptacle, and is therefore eternally prior." But this idea of nothing is, he writes, "a pseudo-idea." He adds, a bit further on, "In a word, whether it be a void of matter or a void of consciousness, *the representation of the void is always a representation which is full and which resolves itself on analysis into two positive elements: the idea, distinct or confused, of a*

substitution, and the feeling, experienced or imagined, of a desire or a regret" (pp. 276–77, 283, author's emphasis). —Trans.

ANNOTATIONS

1. For the text of *Paix et Droit*, see M. Absensour and C. Chalier, eds., *Cahier de l'Herne: Levinas*, no. 60.

2. *Difficult Freedom: Essays on Judaism*, trans. Seán Hand (Baltimore, Md.: Johns Hopkins University Press, 1990).

3. See *Noms propres*, p. 64/45 for the citations on this page.

4. "From the Carefree Deficiency to the New Meaning," in *Of God Who Comes to Mind*, p. 88/46.

5. *Theory of Intuition in Husserl's Phenomenology*, trans. André Orianne (Evanston, Ill: Northwestern University Press, 1995). —Trans.

See note 8 in the introduction and summary that Jean Hering gave of this work of Levinas, in the same issue of the *Revue philosophique* in which Levinas published "Martin Heidegger and Ontology."

6. Levinas, "Transcendence and Evil," first published in the journal *Le Nouveau Commerce* 41 (Autumn 1978), 55–78; see p. 73. [*Collected Philosophical Papers: Levinas*, trans. Alphonso Lingis (Dordrecht: Kluwer Academic Publishers, 1993; rpt. Pittsburgh, Penn.: Duquesne University Press, 1998), pp. 175–86. The present translation appeared in *Of God Who Comes to Mind*, p. 134. —Trans.]

7. Maurice Blanchot, *L'écriture du désastre* (Paris: Gallimard, 1980), p. 40 [*The Writing of the Disaster*, trans. Ann Smock (Lincoln: University of Nebraska Press, 1986, 1995) —Trans.].

8. See OB, p. 187n5 (English translation).

9. The expression is "percer le fond du ciel"; it is found in *Ma mère*, in Bataille, *Œuvres complètes*, vol. 4 (Paris: Gallimard, 1971), p. 269. *My Mother*, trans. Austryn Wainhouse (London: Cape, 1972), pp. 129–30. —Trans.

10. Rolland follows Levinas in hyphenating the term "disaster" in such a way that its meaning approaches the idea of a loss of the guiding star, or magnetic north (i.e., *dés-astre*). Contemporary dis-

aster is precisely the loss of a κοσμος, understood as an order and an Aristotelian hierarchy of being whose imitation was the art of human existing for the Greeks. For Levinas, following Blanchot and his concept of *désastre*, the loss of a fixed point of orientation in the modern age only reveals more clearly the nature of being in its active, verbal self-positing and its anonymous, "dis-heartening hubbub." Also note Levinas's cogent remark from 1976, "For the confluence of philosophical and ethical discourses to be convincing, however, for the order of what has come . . . to be called nature, in its cold splendor or in its scientific and astronomic legality, to take on a meaning for man recognized in his dis-aster, a response must be given to the problem of death." "On Death in the Thought of Ernst Bloch," in *Of God Who Comes to Mind*, p. 35. —Trans.

11. Bataille, *Ma mère*, p. 276/137.

12. Ibid.

13. See Bataille, *Madame Edwarda* in *Œuvres completes*, vol. 3, p. 31. [*My Mother; Madame Edwarda; and The Dead Man; With Essays by Yukio Mishima and Ken Hollings*, trans. Austryn Wainhouse (London: Marion Boyars, 1989, 1995). —Trans.]

14. Hegel writes there, "[Self-consciousness] plunges into life and indulges to the full the pure individuality in which it appears. It does not so much make its own happiness as straightway take it and enjoy it. . . . Its action is only in one respect an action of *desire*. It does not aim at the destruction of objective being in its entirety, but only at the form of its otherness or its independence. . . . " See *Hegel's Phenomenology of Spirit*, trans. A. V. Miller (New York: Oxford University Press, 1977), §§ 361–62, p. 218. —Trans.

15. TI, pp. 4–5.

16. Levinas, "La mauvaise conscience et l'inexorable," first published in French in the journal *Exercises de la patience*, no. 2 (Winter 1981), p. 112. ["Bad Conscience and the Inexorable," in *Of God Who Comes to Mind*, p. 176. —Trans.]

17. Friedrich Nietzsche, *Philosophy in the Tragic Age of the*

Greeks, trans. Marianne Cowan (South Bend, Ind.: Gateway, 1962), §4.

18. "Bad Conscience and the Inexorable," in *Of God Who Comes to Mind*, pp. 174–75.

19. Ibid., p. 175.

20. *Was ist Metaphysik?* 32–33/68/59 [p. 103].

21. See *Recherches philosophiques*, vol. 4 (1934–1935), pp. 392–95.

22. "A Dieu" is a salutation that implies "I commend you to God's care." It carries a finality comparable to the English "farewell." The reference *to* God also contains an abstract directionality and a dative sense, "unto God." —Trans.

23. "Hermeneutics and Beyond," in *Of God Who Comes to Mind*, pp. 109–10.

24. "Philosophie et positivité," in *Savoir, faire espérer: Les limites de la raison* (Brussels: Facultés Universitaires Saint-Louis, 1976), p. 197.

25. See "Philosophie et l'idée de l'infini," which first appeared in *Revue de métaphysique et morale*, no. 3 (Paris: Colin, 1957). Reprinted in *En découvrant l'existence avec Husserl et Heidegger*, p. 166. ["Philosophy and the Idea of the Infinite," in *Discovering Existence with Husserl*, ed. Richard A. Cohen, trans. Michael B. Smith (Evanston, Ill. : Northwestern University Press, 1998). —Trans.]

26. *Paix et Droit*, no. 4 (1935), pp. 6–7.

27. Levinas, *Difficile liberté: Essais sur le judaïsme* (Paris: Albin Michel, 1976, 2d ed.) p. 302. [*Difficult Freedom: Essays on Judaism*, trans. Seán Hand (Baltimore, Md.: Johns Hopkins University, 1990), p. 233. —Trans.]

28. In these sentences the transitive verb "entendre" and the reflexive "s'entendre" mean, respectively, to understand one another to the point of agreement, and to understand in the sense of hearing the meaning. The root *tendere* means to stretch or move toward something; *attendre* and *entendre*, which ran together in Old French, entail, as Rolland knows, the sense of "to turn one's ear, to give auditory attention." In the present case, common sense is rooted in agreement and the understanding based on hearing one

another. Levinas's extensive discussion of "pro-phetism," employed both in a hyphenated and an unhyphenated form, as what encourages speech (*pro-phansis*) and the speaking of ethical fraternity, is like the other side of hearing qua understanding. —Trans.

29. Rolland is playing on the contrast between the West as the land of the evening sun and the East as the land of the morning sun or sunrise. To go to the extreme point in the East would be to venture all the way to the site of the first sunrise. When he says that we are not going astray in a middle East, he does not mean in *today*'s Middle East, which is "Moyen Orient" in French, whereas Rolland writes, "Orient moyen." —Trans.

30. *Humanisme de l'autre homme,* p. 96.

Cultural Memory | *in the Present*

Emmanuel Levinas, *On Escape*

Dan Zahavi, *Husserl's Phenomenology*

Rodolphe Gasché, *The Idea of Form: Rethinking Kant's Aesthetics*

Michael Naas, *Taking on the Tradition: Jacques Derrida and the Legacies of Deconstruction*

Herlinde Pauer-Studer, ed., *Constructions of Practical Reason: Interviews on Moral and Political Philosophy*

Jean-Luc Marion, *Being Given: Toward a Phenomenology of Givenness*

Theodor W. Adorno and Max Horkheimer, *Dialectic of Enlightenment*

Ian Balfour, *The Rhetoric of Romantic Prophecy*

Martin Stokhof, *World and Life as One: Ethics and Ontology in Wittgenstein's Early Thought*

Gianni Vattimo, *Nietzsche: An Introduction*

Jacques Derrida, *Negotiations: Interventions and Interviews, 1971–1998*, ed. Elizabeth Rottenberg

Brett Levinson, *The Ends of Literature: Post-transition and Neoliberalism in the Wake of the "Boom"*

Timothy J. Reiss, *Against Autonomy: Global Dialectics of Cultural Exchange*

Hent de Vries and Samuel Weber, eds., *Religion and Media*

Niklas Luhmann, *Theories of Distinction: Re-Describing the Descriptions of Modernity*, ed. and introd. William Rasch

Johannes Fabian, *Anthropology with an Attitude: Critical Essays*

Michel Henry, *I Am the Truth: Toward a Philosophy of Christianity*

Gil Anidjar, *"Our Place in al-Andalus": Kabbalah, Philosophy, Literature in Arab-Jewish Letters*

Hélène Cixous and Jacques Derrida, *Veils*

F. R. Ankersmit, *Historical Representation*

F. R. Ankersmit, *Political Representation*

Elissa Marder, *Dead Time: Temporal Disorders in the Wake of Modernity (Baudelaire and Flaubert)*

Reinhart Koselleck, *The Practice of Conceptual History: Timing History, Spacing Concepts*

Niklas Luhmann, *The Reality of the Mass Media*

Hubert Damisch, *A Childhood Memory by Piero della Francesca*

Hubert Damisch, *A Theory of /Cloud/: Toward a History of Painting*